THE PRICE OF LEISURE

THE PRICE OF LEISURE

*An Economic Analysis of the Demand
for Leisure Time*

JOHN D. OWEN

Assistant Professor, The Johns Hopkins University

With a Foreword by

J. MINCER

Professor of Economics, Columbia University

1970

McGILL-QUEEN'S UNIVERSITY PRESS

MONTREAL

ISBN 0 7735 0094 4

ACKNOWLEDGMENTS

Professors Jacob Mincer and Gary Becker of Columbia University gave many hours of their time in reading and discussing with me an earlier version of this manuscript. The members of the Columbia University Labor Workshop, especially Edwin Dean, offered many useful criticisms. The present manuscript was prepared at the Johns Hopkins University where I benefited from the comments of Professors Carl Christ and Edwin Mills.

I would like to express my appreciation of the financial support received over a two-year period from the Ford Foundation to carry on this research. A grant from the Rosenthal Foundation paid for much of the computing and typing that was required.

Unpublished data on hours and wages received from Professor John Kendrick of the National Bureau of Economic Research enabled me to carry out the empirical analyses presented in the text.

Finally, I want to acknowledge the services of Mrs. V. E. Nilsson, whose typing work over the last two years has been uniformly excellent.

FOREWORD

Dr. Owen's study represents a significant contribution to the rapidly developing research in the field of labor supply. Conceptually, the study represents a link between the traditional and the innovative: following Lionel Robbins, the supply of a worker's time to the labor market is treated as the obverse of his demand for non-working or 'leisure' time. With this starting point, Owen goes on to introduce substantive content to the notion of non-working time, specifically in terms of recreational activities. It soon becomes clear, of course, that recreation is but one of many uses of consumption time, though it is particularly important in Owen's application. Consequently, the demand for non-working time is a demand derived from the demand for consumption activities, such as recreation. And the study of labor supply becomes a special case of a generalized approach to the theory of consumption. This approach has been a focus of research of the Workshop in Labor Economics at Columbia University, in which Owen was an active participant. Its full theoretical exposition is contained in Professor Gary Becker's well known article on 'A Theory of Allocation of Time' in the *Economic Journal* of September 1965.

In his empirical implementation of this generalized 'consumption' approach to the study of labor supply, Owen attempts a direct econometric estimation of the determinants of secularly and cyclically changing hours of work in the U.S. since 1900. Whether in econometric specification or in less formal analysis, the conceptual framework prompts a range of fascinating considerations, such as the relevance of changes in education, working conditions, unemployment, and transportation to work. However one measures the success of this pioneering venture, it will lead the way to more intensive exploration in this important area.

In this short introduction I cannot give full justice to the range of ideas and questions which Owen either confronts or provokes in the reader's mind. I am confident that these ideas and questions will continue to occupy the time of students of labor economics at Columbia and elsewhere.

July, 1969   JACOB MINCER

TABLE OF CONTENTS

CHAPTER 1

INTRODUCTION

1.1 MAIN PURPOSES OF THIS STUDY

This study presents a new approach to the analysis of the demand for leisure time. Traditionally, economic analysis of the income-leisure choice has been carried out almost entirely in terms of the effects on time spent at work, of changes in the real hourly wage rate, or of changes in the tax structure. The study of leisure time itself is emphasized in the present work, and the analysis is broadened to consider the role played in the determination of leisure time by such factors as: the development of the commercial recreation industry, fatigue, education, commuting, working conditions, productive consumption and unemployment.

In the first section (Chapter 2) an analysis is presented of the relationship of the demand for leisure time to each of these factors. In addition to a more conventional, static analysis, an attempt is made here to understand some of the relationships between economic development and the income-leisure choice. Hence, an analysis is given of how the determinants of the demand for leisure time will be affected by economic development and of how such changes in the explanatory variables will in turn change the demand for leisure time. Thus, rising real wage rates, the development of a commercial recreation industry, urbanization, the proliferation of educational opportunities, the development of a modern system of government finance, and other results of economic progress are each studied to predict their impact on the demand for leisure time.

For example, it is argued here that the development of the commercial recreation industry, accompanied by reductions in the relative price of recreation, will increase the demand for leisure time, if leisure time and commercial recreation are complementary.

In the second part of the book (Chapters 3-5), an empirical verifi-

1

cation is attempted of some of the notions presented in Chapter 2. An attempt is made here to include the relative price of recreation, unemployment, and fatigue, as well as the real hourly wage rate, as explanatory variables in the determination of the demand for leisure time. The relationship between leisure and recreation is examined further by estimating the demand for market recreation as a function of the price of leisure as well as in the more conventional way.

Time series of leisure time for the United States, 1900-1961, are developed from data on hours of work and vacations and holidays presented in Chapter 3. Recreation price and quantity data are analyzed in Chapter 4. These data are used in the statistical work presented in Chapter 5. (Chapters 3 and 4 may be omitted by the reader who wishes to go directly from the economic analysis of Chapter 2 to the empirical models and regression results of Chapter 5.)

In section 5.1, a number of empirical models are developed to estimate the demand for leisure time as a function of income, the price of leisure, and the price of market recreation. In several of these, synthetic variables are constructed in order to obtain a more appropriate model. For example, the conventional measure of real income (money income divided by a price index) reflects the choice of a level of leisure time and thus may not be suitable to use as an independent variable in the estimation of leisure time. Hence, in one set of regressions, real income is measured by adding leisure time to the conventional measure of income (and then by deflating this measure by a price index which includes the price of leisure). In several regressions the unemployment rate is used as a determinant of the marginal price of leisure. Estimates of output-reducing fatigue were also constructed and are used to measure the marginal price of leisure.

In sections 5.2 and 5.3, a two-equation model is developed in order to test for bias in the regression results of section 5.1. This model adds an employer demand for labor equation to the original demand for leisure time function.

The relationship between the demand for leisure time and commercial recreation is then explored further by estimating the demand for market recreation as a function of the relative price of leisure (section 5.4); by forming a composite variable, leisure activity, from leisure time and market recreation and estimating its demand (section 5.5); and, finally, by estimating the elasticity of substitution between leisure time and market recreation.

2

It is necessary to state clearly the sense in which the term 'leisure time' will be used in this study. The concept of what constitutes leisure time has changed over the years, reflecting changes in our ways of thinking about man and his free time, as well as changes in the social structure itself.

Thus, the present notion of leisure time is quite different from the Aristotelian view. Aristotle distinguished true leisure from amusement. Leisure or free time was the basis of contemplation, of true happiness:

And happiness is thought to depend on leisure; for we are busy that we may have leisure, and make war that we may live in peace.[1]

Amusement, correctly used, serves to refresh for further exertion:

Happiness, therefore, doesn't lie in amusement; it would indeed be strange if the end were amusement; and one were to take trouble and suffer hardship all one's life in order to amuse oneself ... Now to exert oneself and work for the sake of amusement seems silly and utterly childish. But to amuse oneself in order that one may exert oneself, as Anarchis put it, seems right; for amusement is a sort of relaxation, and we need relaxation because we can not work continuously. Relaxation, then, is not an end; for it is taken for the sake of activity.[2]

The Aristotelian view of leisure has come under attack in modern times on the grounds that contemplation *is not* leisure and that amusement *is* leisure.

According to Josef Pieper, a contemporary Swiss Catholic philosopher, the first challenge (that contemplation is not leisure) is based on the Kantian view that understanding is the product of work. He describes the change in these words:

Knowledge, man's spiritual, intellectual knowledge (such is Kant's thesis) is activity, exclusively activity. Working on that basis, Kant was bound to reach the view that knowing and philosophizing (philosophizing in particu-

1. ARISTOTLE, *The Nichomachean Ethics*, trans. H. Rackham (N.Y.: G.P. Putnam's Sons, 1926), Book X, Chapter 7.
2. ARISTOTLE, *ibid.*, Book X, Chapter 6.

3

lar, since it is furthest removed from purely physical awareness) must be regarded and understood as *work*.[3]

The philosophers of antiquity thought otherwise on this matter ... the Greeks – Aristotle no less than Plato – as well as the great medieval thinkers, held that not only physical, sensuous perception, but equally man's spiritual and intellectual knowledge, included an element of pure receptive contemplation, or, as Heraclitus says, of 'listening to the essence of things'.[4]

The Aristotelian view is also criticized or rejected altogether on the grounds that amusement, or recreation, should be considered as leisure. Maxim Gorky puts this point most strongly when he says, 'The only true leisure is rest from work.'

Although many of us would not admit to holding such a puritanical view of leisure, most writers, including myself, are influenced by it, at least to the extent of regarding leisure as time not spent at work, and by putting recreational activities at the center of their discussion of leisure.

The view of leisure as time not spent at work is reinforced by two tendencies: first, changes in the economic and social structure which have led to the virtual absence of an aristocratic leisure class in the United States, and, second, the concern of social studies with the behavior of broad strata of population rather than with that of narrowly based elites.

In the present work, for example, most of the empirical and analytical results are obtained from a study of the behavior of wage and salary workers in nonagricultural industries in the United States. It is concerned with their choice between income and leisure and thus requires a definition of leisure which will somehow give meaning to this choice.

For these several reasons then, leisure is equated with consumption time, where consumption time is defined as time devoted to activities which are, at the margin, primarily carried on for their own sake (consumption activities),[5] rather than for the control over financial or other resources which the activity might yield. In practice, this means the exclusion from consumption time of market employment and of household production. In modern urban conditions the household production

3. Josef PIEPER, *Leisure the Basis of Culture*, trans. Alexander Dru (N.Y.: Pantheon Books, 1952), p. 32.
4. PIEPER, *ibid.*, p. 33.
5. For this definition to be usable in practice, we have to look at a leisure-time

4

of an individual would include, along with his housework, do-it-yourself repairs, and the time spent in commuting and, possibly, in the personal care necessary to hold his job. All these activities, then, are excluded from the leisure category.

However, this concept of leisure time as consumption time does include in the leisure category time spent in certain activities which are essential as well as gratifying, such as sleeping and eating. [6] This definition of leisure is analogous to a definition of food consumption which includes the bare essentials of diet, or, in fact, to one of disposable income as a measure of consumer income.

An alternative approach would be to define leisure as 'free time', which would be analogous to the market research concept of 'discretionary income' (income over and above some subsistence level). One might then measure leisure as that time devoted to recreation and (non-productive) contemplation. But just as those definitions of subsistence income used in measuring discretionary income characteristically show it as well above that level actually required to sustain life, so the time spent on eating and sleeping is in excess of that required for survival.[7] Total eating and sleeping time might well account for an important segment of free time.

The definition of leisure time as consumption time emphasizes the subjective intent with which an activity is approached, rather than the objective purpose which it serves. This concept of leisure time ignores, then, the various external effects of consumption activities. For example, the survival of the American republic (and, in this nuclear age, the

activity as a whole. For example, for a beginner the first days on the ski slope might be quite unpleasant and endured only in order to enjoy later days on the slope as an accomplished skier. Thus the whole period 'skiing' would be the unit of measurement. For some purposes one might include transportation to and from the activity as part of the activity.

6. As long as the marginal unit of time devoted to the activity is not essential.

7. Leisurely eating and sleeping is less important in the United States than in some other countries. (But see Margaret MEAD, 'The Pattern of Leisure in Contemporary American Culture', *Annals of the American Academy of Political and Social Science*, CCCXIII (1957), 11-15, for important instances in our culture. See also the time budgets presented as Table 4-A on p. 82 of this study. Among the unemployed, both men and women spend more time eating and sleeping than do laborers, housewives, white-collar workers, professionals, and executives. The only exception to this is that white-collar males spend more time eating than do unemployed males.)

survival of the world) may depend upon whether reading of serious news analyses is as attractive a pursuit to the tired American worker or businessman as is watching televised ice hockey.

However, the external effects of an individual worker's political knowledge will not, if they are truly external, affect his income,[8] and thus they would come under the heading of consumption, rather than that of work time.

When the private rather than the public purposes for which activities are pursued is stressed, and when the emphasis is placed upon the purpose for which an activity is carried on at the margin rather than upon its contribution to subsistence, leisure time or consumption time is seen to occupy a large place in the time budget. In the empirical analysis of the allocation of time of employed, nonstudent American males presented in Table 4-A, about 90 percent of time not spent in market employment comes under this heading.

1.3 A POSSIBLE CONTRADICTION BETWEEN THE CONCEPT OF THE INCOME-LEISURE CHOICE AND THAT OF LEISURE AS A CONSUMER GOOD

The use of consumer theory to analyze the demand for leisure time must be made cautiously. These consumption activities are defined as those which are (on the margin, at least) chosen for themselves, rather than for money; leisure time is the time spent in consumption activities. Does this definition, then, involve an implicit assumption that more leisure time as such is desired by the consumer?

It is a commonplace that the ceremonial meal(s) of the day is often time-consuming and economically inefficient in societies which are passing from a preindustrial to an industrial state. Variations in sleep patterns are less well known. Nelson N. Foote writes: 'Patterns of sleeping vary widely, both as to duration and frequency of sleeping. Anthropologists who have studied natives of the South Pacific, where the nearest to completely leisured societies exist, report that sleep is so interspersed throughout the day and mingled with routine activities that it would show frequencies incredibly high and durations incredibly short by our standards, yet with total duration probably much higher'. 'Methods for Study of Meaning in Use of Time', in *Aging and Leisure*, ed. R. W. KLEEMEIER (New York: Oxford University Press, 1961), pp. 162-63.
8. Although collectively the political knowledge of the electorate may influence wages (e.g., by changing the rate of economic progress).

6

The answer depends upon whether the choice is between leisure time and no time, or between leisure time and work time. A critical distinction must be made here between the economic analysis of time and that of money. The economist knows that money, or the goods and services purchased for consumer activities with money, are desired by the consumer. The simplest proof of this is that the consumer may dispose of money at approximately zero cost, if he is so inclined, rather than use it to make purchases.

But do people prefer more consumption time to less, at the same level of money income? This is a much more dubious proposition, since we cannot destroy time in bits and pieces like so many dollar bills. As long as we exist, we have 'time'. In fact, one might conceive of reformulating the leisure-no leisure choice as that between more or less existence.[9]

Economic analysis of the income-leisure choice tells us that, in equilibrium, the utility-maximizing worker-consumer will prefer a level of hours of work such that the marginal utility of an hour of work plus the marginal utility of the income earned in an additional hour's work (i.e., the wage rate times the marginal utility of income) equals the marginal utility of an hour of leisure.

This equality implies that, as long as the income earned in an hour's work yields positive utility, the marginal utility of leisure will be greater than the marginal utility of work. But this requirement is quite consistent with an equilibrium in which the marginal utilities of leisure and work are either both positive or both negative, as well as with the more conventional situation in which the marginal utility of leisure is positive, and the marginal utility of work, negative. Thus, just as it is possible for one man to love his work, but to love his leisure more, another man may hate his job, and be bored even more by his leisure.[10]

In other words, the reason why an individual will prefer to spend more consumption time rather than less at an activity may be that it kills time, rather than that he enjoys it.[11]

9. But see p. 8 for a logical objection to this reformulation.
10. At least, at his present level of income. The marginal utility of leisure may rise with income so that, at high levels of income, the marginal utility of leisure becomes positive.
11. This need not lead to suicide. Apart from other considerations, an individual may like the first fifteen hours a day of consumption time and hate the sixteenth. And he may like the first seven hours of work and hate the eighth. Thus the total utility of time to him may be positive, while the marginal utility of an hour is negative.

Some light might be shed on the question of whether individuals prefer leisure to no leisure by observing the circumstances under which they take measures to prolong life (not smoking, saving for one's old age), and under what conditions they take measures to shorten it (suicide, smoking).[12] However, apart from the psychological and institutional restraints placed on these aspects of human behavior by society, there are the logical objections that on the one hand, the prolongation of life in the prime working years usually involves the possibility of further work (and thus of more income as well as of more leisure) and, on the other hand, that time made available when one is unable to work because of age or illness may not be as attractive as leisure time enjoyed when one is youthful and fit. These problems of evaluating leisure as such arise (whether or not they are recognized) whenever economists must advise the government as to the desirability of spending large sums to prolong the lives of those who are no longer 'economically productive'.

But the main focus of the present study is on the demand for leisure time in the more conventional sense, and hence the work-leisure choice will be the most relevant one.

Here, it would seem that it will be acceptable to analyze the demand for leisure time as the demand for a consumer good, as long as it is recognized that what is being 'purchased' is not simply an hour of leisure, but rather the substitution of an hour of leisure for an hour of work.[13]

1.4 THE DEMAND FOR LEISURE TIME: LABOR FORCE PARTICIPATION, HOURS OF WORK, VACATIONS AND HOLIDAYS

An empirical analysis of changes in the income-leisure choice made by American workers must confront at the outset the variation in the modes by which leisure preferences are expressed. Larger amounts of consumption time may be obtained at the expense of work time by reducing the number of work hours per day or week, of work weeks

12. Alternatively one might think of the leisure-no leisure choice as that between consciousness and unconsciousness and thus analyze the use of stimulants or of drugs that claim to 'expand consciousness'. But this would be somewhat artificial, since unconsciousness also requires resources to sustain life.
13. Thus, working conditions will be regarded as a determinant of the demand for leisure time.

8

per year, or of working years in one's lifetime.[14] Increases in weekly or annual leisure time are accomplished by reducing hours of work and increasing the level of vacations and holidays, respectively; an increase in the proportion of years worked in one's lifetime usually requires changes in the labor force participation rate.[15]

The contribution of changes in the labor force participation rate to the demand for leisure time is difficult to evaluate. In the past sixty years there have been three major changes in the labor force participation rate: an increase in the female labor force participation rate, a reduction in the participation rate of young males because of the trend toward remaining in school longer, and a reduction in the participation rate of the elderly as they choose or are forced to leave the labor force.[16] However, it is not clear that the first two of these shifts, at least, made an important net contribution to consumption time.

As wages in the United States rose in this century for both men and women, there was a tendency for women to enter the labor force. This movement has been explained in terms of the higher opportunity cost to women of staying home. [17] It became more efficient for a woman to take a job, often part-time, and to use part of the proceeds to purchase prepared household goods or appliances which save time in housework.

There is little reason to believe, however, that this change has led to a net decrease in the amount of leisure enjoyed by the average woman. On the contrary, since an increase in the general level of wages of males has been associated with an increase in their leisure time, one might guess that the same would be true for women.

Empirical data on female leisure-work patterns are much inferior to those on males, since a smaller portion of female work is done in the market. However, empirical analyses of the allocation of time by men and women indicate that the leisure patterns of the two sexes are rather

14. Or by taking measures to extend one's life span. This possibility is not considered here, although it may have relevance to some of the questions examined. See section 1.3 above.

15. An exception would arise with a prolonged sabbatical leave.

16. This combines with the higher proportion of aged in the population to account for the larger percentage of non-working elderly males in the population.

17. J. MINCER, 'Labor Force Participation of Married Women: A Study of Labor Supply', in *Aspects of Labor Economics*. National Bureau of Economic Research Special Conference Series, No. 14; A Conference of the Universities-National Bureau Committee for Economic Research (Princeton: Princeton University Press, 1962). For a more detailed discussion of this subject, see G. G. CAIN, *Married Women in the Labor Force* (Chicago: University of Chicago Press, 1966).

similar. Two time budget studies, one for 1932, the other for 1950, are shown in Table 4-A, pp. 82-83. In the earlier study, at least, housewives appear to work fewer hours than men, and working women, somewhat longer hours.

As the age at which young people leave school rises, the labor force participation rates of males in age group fourteen to twenty-four years decline. This might usefully be regarded as a choice of leisure over work if school work required fewer hours than did conventional employment, or if it were so preferred over work that the rate of return on education were driven well below that of other investment.

Time budgets indicate that average work-leisure patterns of students and young workers are quite similar. Financial rates of return on the investment of time in high school and college have been given considerable attention in recent years. These rates have been found to be as high as or higher than rates on conventional investments.

These high financial returns may reflect imperfections in the capital market.[18] Hence one can only say that the evidence does not indicate a rejection of the hypothesis that later entrance into the labor force reflects only a change in the nature of work done (analogous perhaps to the shift from blue-collar to white-collar work in its effects on the choice between labor and leisure).

Undoubtedly, the earlier retirement age and longer life span which enables (or forces) the average American worker to spend a number of years in idleness at the end of his life yields an addition to his total consumption or leisure time. There is considerable controversy in the literature as to the extent to which this leisure is enforced, either by the difficulty that the aged face in finding employment, or by the danger that continued working will hasten sickness or death.

It is probable that a large part of the increase in retirements from the labor force [19] can be accounted for by the higher income that the employee has at his disposal, including pensions, savings, and, perhaps, a

18. E.g., a family may have a rate of discount of future income of 25 percent but still send a son to college at a rate of return of 12 percent if the parents believe that the boy will enjoy it more than work. But the rate of return is still a better guide for our purpose than the attitudes of the students towards the relative pleasures of work and study. The financial rate of return would be driven down if schooling were largely a preparation for the enjoyment of leisure time, even if the learning process itself were a very painful one.

19. Actual retirement from the labor force may only come several years after the worker has been fired or pensioned from the job he has had for most of his life.

portion of the higher income of his children. This income enables him to stop working, either because he voluntarily chooses leisure time over work time, or, more commonly, because he is now removed from the desperation that fifty years ago would have forced him to work on at the expense of his health (i.e., although he may prefer leisure time to sickness or death, he may not prefer it to work as such).

In any event, while the changing pattern of life span and retirement age has increased the amount of time available for consumption, it is not clear that it has increased the proportion of time spent in consumption or leisure. Table 1-A shows that there has been but a small decline from 1900 to 1960 in the fraction of his lifetime that a man works for hire. This decline might be eliminated altogether if the data were adjusted for the increase in the number of years of school completed of the average member of the labor force in that period: about six years.[20]

TABLE 1-A

Reductions in per capita work time, U.S. males, 1900-1960

U.S. males	1900	1960
1. Hours of work per week *	58.5	41.0
2. Total years of life, expected at birth †	48.2	66.6
3. Years in labor force, expected at birth †	32.1	41.4
4. Years out of labor force, expected at birth †	16.1	25.2
5. Proportion of week spent in market employment: (1)/168	0.348	0.245
6. Proportion of life spent in labor force: (3)/(2)	0.666	0.622
7. Proportion of life spent at work: (5)×(6)	0.234	0.152

* Source: Table 3-A, p. 67, below.
† Source: Seymour Wolfbein, *Changing Patterns of Working Life*, p. 10.

Thus, one must conclude that, while the various changes in labor force participation rates and in the age structure of the population may have had significant effects on the aggregate consumption of leisure time, they have partially canceled each other. In any event, the net effect of these several changes is quite difficult to isolate.[21]

20. For some purposes an absolute rather than a proportionate measure of lifetime consumption time might be preferred. But the data *must* be converted into the proportionate form if they are to be compared with data on hours of work per week or with annual per capita income in an analysis of the labor-leisure choice.
21. These remarks apply only to time series of aggregate consumption time. Some

A much less ambiguous method of providing increased leisure time has been by reducing hours of work and by increasing vacations and holidays. In the last sixty years, hours of work per male worker have declined by almost one-third. In the postwar years, the more traditional method of increasing leisure time by reducing weekly hours has been supplemented by a great proliferation of vacations and holidays among the labor force.

Thus, while leisure time per capita has probably been influenced by the various trends in labor force participation, reduction in hours per year has been the principal method of creating more leisure time for American employees in the twentieth century. Moreover, it has been the least complicated way, and hence the most suitable for empirical analysis.[22]

1.5 INSTITUTIONS OF HOURS DETERMINATION IN THE UNITED STATES

The market for work time in the United States is analyzed in Chapter 2, and an attempt is made to determine which variables are most suitable for an empirical explanation of changes in the level of leisure time. Such factors as the real wage rate, the relative price of recreation, the fatigue associated with long hours, and the level of unemployment in the labor market are considered likely to be important in the determination of the work week.

This explanation of hours of leisure and hours of work in terms of real income and relative prices implies that, at least in times of full employment, hours of work generally reflect the leisure preferences of the individuals making up the community. But some economists would

very interesting work has been done, for example, in isolating the effects of economic variables in cross-sectional analyses of labor force participation rates. See MINCER, 'Labor Force Participation of Married Women'.

22. Cf. discussions of reductions in hours of work and in labor force participation as alternative ways of increasing leisure time, in H.G. LEWIS, 'Hours of Work and Hours of Leisure', in *Proceedings of Ninth Annual Meeting of Industrial Relations Research Association* (Cleveland: Industrial Relations Research Association, 1957), and in C.D. LONG, *The Labor Force Under Changing Income and Employment* (National Bureau of Economic Research General Series, No. 65; Princeton: Princeton University Press, 1958).

insist that the institutions of hours determination today are not those of a free market, and that the influence of the state, of the trade unions, or of other groups is such that a demand analysis developed from a theory of free choice is inappropriate.

An explanation of the demand for leisure time in terms of market variables does not, of course, imply that employers do permit each employee to set his own hours. Within a factory there are compelling reasons for imposing standard hours on groups of employees. Moreover, there is some empirical evidence that hours of work in many industries are almost completely standardized now and that, taking the nation as a whole, there has been a trend towards standardization of hours since the turn of the century or earlier.[23]

However, the analysis of the demand for leisure in terms of market variables does seem to imply that the employer is free to change hours schedules when the leisure preferences of his employees change.[24] This view is challenged by the existence of widespread state regulation of hours and by the unionization of about one-third of all employees in the United States.

Insofar as the union or state reflects the individual preference of the employee, there may be merely a substitution of state or union official for employer as a reflector of employee attitudes. In that case, the level of leisure time would continue to reflect individual preferences. However, apart from the distortions produced by the inherently bureaucratic nature of decision-making by state agencies or by trade unions,[25] such organizations would not be expected to reflect the pref-

23. John OWEN, 'Reduction in Hours in the U.S. 1900-1957' (unpublished Master's thesis, Department of Economics, New York University, 1959). It is argued there that the standardization that exists may be due in part to a 'taste for standardization' of leisure hours (arising, e.g., from a desire to see friends or to watch certain television programs) on the part of the employees themselves. See M. A. BIENEFELD, 'The Normal Week Under Collective Bargaining', *Economica*, XXXVI, No. 142 (May, 1969), 172-92, for a recent discussion of the relationship between the social environment and the demand for leisure time.

24. As A. C. PIGOU points out (in his *Economics of Welfare*, 1st edition; London: Macmillan and Co., 1920), it is inappropriate to describe hours determination under this system as an example of 'individual bargaining' since the employer generally sets a level of hours for his shop. Employees can either accept it or quit. Hours determination is thus distinguished from wage determination in the unorganized shop, since some scope is allowed there for individual (often secret) bargaining on wage rates.

25. But see PIGOU, *ibid.*, for the distortions (often bureaucratic) inherent in the system of employer-dominated hours determination.

13

erences of individuals as such, but rather those of some group (e.g., the union might reflect the interests of members, the state that of the citizens). And the collective interest of the group need not of course be equal to the sum of the individual interests.

Thus, state regulators have often taken the position that a man or child should be restrained from 'selling his health for wages'[26] by working long hours. Another factor in state regulation today is of course the 'share-the-work' theory behind the Fair Labor Standards Act and other hours limits spawned by widespread unemployment. In this theory, an extension of hours of work of employees does not mean an increase in production but simply a number of layoffs, and thus an increase in the number of unemployed.

Moreover, trade unions must act in the knowledge that they are facing downward-sloping demand curves for their product, labor. Thus, a reduction by one in hours worked by all members of the union will typically lead to a loss per member in labor income that is less than average hourly earnings.[27] One would guess that this situation would provide a spur to shorter hours.[28]

Thus, the spread of unionization and of state hours laws could have a downward effect on hours of work.

However, empirical work has not supported the hypothesis that the changing institutions of hours determination have had a very important downward influence on average hours of work of all employees in the United States in the twentieth century.[29]

Investigators have pointed out that until the passage of the Fair Labor Standards Act most workers were not covered by hours laws and that, where they were covered, they were usually working at schedules below the state maximum. Yet the more dramatic reductions in hours

26. Though the wages be spent on food, housing, medicine. But we are concerned here with the theory that motivates state regulation, not with the effects of regulation (see section 2.7, 'Productive Consumption and the Demand for Leisure Time', below).
27. This will hold even if the union only controls a section of the industry. As long as there is a positively-sloped supply curve of labor to the industry, a restriction on hours in the union sector should lead to some increase in the hourly wage rate.
28. Since the effect is to reduce the price of leisure, the empirical results shown in Chapter 5, indicating a negative relationship between the price of leisure and hours of leisure, give further substance to this point.
29. Although they can not rule out the possibility that such changes have had important effects on individual industries or areas.

14

of work in the United States occurred before the passage of the Fair Labor Standards Act.

Moreover, while the Fair Labor Standards Act brought about a short-term reduction in hours of work in those industries where it was applied, there is some evidence that, in the years following the passage of the F.L.S.A., reductions in hours were larger in industries not covered by the act than in covered industries.[30] Thus, at least part of the initial effect of the F.L.S.A. was eroded in subsequent years.

Again, while unions have reduced hours schedules in many industries, this reduction is due in part to the raises in wages that they achieve, in part to the fact that the union, unlike the individual employee, faces a downward-sloping demand curve. Two investigations which attempted to find some influence of unions on hours beyond that yielded by the rise in wages the unions obtained were unsuccessful.[31]

Finally, several empirical studies (including this one) which have analyzed hours of work in the United States have been able to account for a large part of the movement in aggregate hours without recourse to an explanation in terms of changes in the institutions of hours determination.[32]

When the actual course of hours change in the United States is examined (see Chapter 3), it does seem that these institutions have had some effect on the short-run timing of hours change. One might conclude tentatively, then, that the changes in institutions of hours determination in the United States have been conducive to shorter hours, but that the influence of such factors on hours of work has been less important in long-term movements than in short-run changes.

30. H.G. LEWIS, 'Hours of Work and Hours of Leisure.'
31. Ethel JONES, 'Hours of Work in the U.S., 1900-1957' (unpublished Ph.D. dissertation, University of Chicago, 1959); and T.A. FINEGAN, 'Hours of Work in the United States, A Cross-Sectional Analysis' (unpublished Ph.D. dissertation, University of Chicago, 1960).
32. Ethel JONES, ibid.

CHAPTER 2

AN ECONOMIC ANALYSIS OF THE DEMAND FOR

LEISURE TIME

2.1 THE DEMAND FOR LEISURE TIME AND THE WAGE RATE

In the United States most adult males between the ages of twenty-five and sixty-four years work for a living. They sell a large portion of their waking time for wages in industry and support themselves and their families on the proceeds.

This industrial economy is different from earlier societies in several ways relevant to the demand for leisure time. For example, in an industrial economy the seasons of the year are much less important in determining the productivity of labor and thus the distribution of labor time over the course of a year than they are in an agricultural or a pastoral society. In an agricultural society it is natural to work very long hours during the harvest and plowing seasons, for example, and to be much less active in the winter months.

Moreover, our society is relatively secular, so that it makes some sense to talk about the number and timing of holidays as being determined by individual consumer and producer choice, rather than by tradition or by a sacerdotal class.[1]

Finally, the analysis of the income-leisure choice of the working population of the United States is quite different from that of a Greek slaveholder, or of a Renaissance merchant or nobleman. The great bulk of the average nonagricultural employee's income is from wages rather than from property.

Therefore, most modern economic analysis of the determination of hours of work or of leisure time has been in terms of the influence of the wage rate.

Economists have differed in their assessment of net effect of wage changes on the demand for leisure. Adam Smith stressed the productive

1. But see section 1.5, 'Institutions of Hours Determination in the United States', above.

consumption results of a wage increase on labor supply. In the *Wealth of Nations* [2] he states:

The liberal reward of labor increases the industry of the common people... Plentiful subsistence increases the bodily strength of the laborer, and the comfortable hope of bettering his condition and of ending his days, perhaps in ease and plenty, animates him to exert that strength to the utmost.

Marshall agreed with Smith on the long-run effects of a wage change on effort but felt that in the short run the analysis was more complicated. He also recognized a distinction between work time and effort and stressed the demand for leisure time as such.

A man is on duty, bound to be ready when wanted, but perhaps not doing an hour's actual work in the day, and yet he will object to very long hours of duty because they deprive his life of a variety of opportunities for domestic or social pleasures, and perhaps of comfortable meals and rest.

Marshall was not sure as to the short-run outcome of an increase in wages: [3]

It depends then on the individual, whether, with growing pay new wants arise, and new desires to provide comforts for others or for himself in after-years, or he is soon satiated with those enjoyments that can be gained only by work and then craves more rest, and more opportunities for activities that are themselves pleasurable.

The twentieth-century neoclassical economists Knight [4] and Pigou,[5] however, were sure that a wage increase would decrease hours of work. They argued that with higher wages the marginal utility of money would decline, while that of work remained unchanged; an hours cut would then be required to restore equilibrium. This position was soon demolished by Lionel Robbins,[6] who, by stressing the price effect of an increase in wages (i.e., the fact that an increase in wages reduces the 'effort price of income' or raises the money price of leisure), showed the indeterminacy of the hours-wage rate relationship.

2. Adam SMITH, *Wealth of Nations* (N.Y.: Modern Library, 1937), p. 81.
3. Alfred MARSHALL, *Principles of Economics*, 8th ed. (London: Macmillan and Co., Ltd., 1920), pp. 527-29.
4. Frank H. KNIGHT, *Risk, Uncertainty and Profit* (Boston: Houghton Mifflin and Co., 1921), pp. 117-18.
5. A.C. PIGOU, *A Study in Public Finance* (London: Macmillan and Co., Ltd., 1928), pp. 83-84.
6. Lionel ROBBINS, 'On the Elasticity of Income in Terms of Effort', *Economics*, X (June, 1930), 123-29.

Since the Robbins article appeared, economists have agreed that the effect on leisure of an increase in the wage rate is indeterminate.[7] An increase in property income will, if we assume leisure is a superior good, reduce hours of work. A higher wage rate also brings higher income which, in itself, may incline the individual to increase his leisure. But at the same time the higher wage rate makes leisure time more expensive in terms of foregone goods and services, so that the individual may decide instead to purchase less leisure. The net effect will depend then on the relative strengths of the income and price elasticities.

All economists can say is that, in view of the history of rising wages and increasing leisure in so many western nations in the past century, it would seem that for the average worker the income effect of a rise in the wage rate is in fact stronger than the substitution effect.

2.2 THE PRICE OF LEISURE: THE APPLICABILITY OF CONSUMER DEMAND ANALYSIS TO THE DEMAND FOR LEISURE TIME

The analysis of the income-leisure choice in terms of the income and substitution effects of a wage change is, of course, quite similar to the analysis of the consumer demand for a good or service.[8]

However, as the analysis proceeds to somewhat more complicated questions in the determination of the demand for leisure time, it becomes important to see to what extent it is appropriate to apply the tools of standard consumer demand analysis to the income-leisure choice.

Leisure time is analogous to a consumer good in several ways. First,

7. This analysis is formally incorporated into the Slutsky-Hicks equations of consumer demand in an article by Gilbert and Pfouts (F. L. GILBERT and R. L. PFOUTS, 'A Theory of the Responsiveness of Hours of Work to Changes in the Wage Rate', *Review of Economics and Statistics*, XL (May, 1958), 116-21). G. S. Becker's analysis of leisure activity (see G. S. BECKER, 'A Theory of the Allocation of Time', *The Economic Journal*, LXXV (September, 1965), 493-517) also yields an indeterminate relationship between wage rate and hours of work. However, time series analyses have shown a negative relationship between income and hours of work. A similar result was found by Finegan, *op. cit.*, in a cross-sectional analysis of hours of work in the United States, and by Winston (Gordon C. WINSTON, 'An International Comparison of Income and Hours of Work', *Review of Economics and Statistics*, XLVIII, No. 1 (February, 1966), 28-39).

8. Except that the consumer in the work-leisure problem is selling his time, not buying it.

the decline in hours of work and the increase in leisure time that we have observed has contributed to the well-being of the nation. It is frequently suggested that increases in leisure time should be measured and should be added to national income to provide a better indicator of economic progress.

Second, leisure does have a price, and changes in its price will affect the demand for it. (What may be the simplest demonstration of this statement is the reaction of workers who are offered double the hourly wage for overtime work.)

In some of the empirical work in this study (see section 5.1) these notions were developed by the addition of leisure time to money income, and by the inclusion of the price of leisure in a consumer price index.

But in some respects the market for leisure time is quite different than that for other consumer goods. In the first place, workers do not buy leisure time – the most that can be said is that they decline to sell it. More important, it is not true that a worker is able to sell all his hours of leisure or consumption time without affecting his average hourly earnings.[9] This contrasts with his purchases of individual consumer goods,[10] which he may reduce to zero without influencing their price.

This dependence of average hourly earnings on hours has a bearing, of course, on the relation of hours of work to the wage rate. An underlying assumption of the simple analysis is that the labor market operates in such a fashion that if the workers in a community wish to work longer hours, they will be able to obtain proportionate gains in money income.[11]

But in fact there are circumstances under which one may obtain increasing returns or economies of scale to work, and others in which diminishing returns will set in. These conditions will alter the price of leisure relative to income and would thus be expected to affect the income-leisure choice. Thus, a crucial part of the analysis of the in-

9. The term 'price of leisure' is reserved to denote the increment of income from an additional hour of work.
10. But if he reduces his consumption of certain *classes* of consumer goods (e.g., food) he will raise the effort or time price required to obtain them (see below, section 2.7, 'Productive Consumption and the Demand for Leisure Time').
11. No one would insist that each individual sets his own hours, but it is argued that the typical employer may be indifferent to the level of hours in his plant.

come-leisure choice is the study of the determination of the price of leisure.

Diminishing returns to work and their effect on the supply of labor have been discussed in work on the economics of taxation, particularly in relation to the progressive income tax. But diminishing or increasing returns to work also exist as a result of the presence of output-reducing fatigue (or productive consumption in consumption time); productive consumption; commuting; education; and, for some people, unemployment. The existence of these conditions will affect the demand for leisure time. The fact that most or all of them have changed in relative importance over the years has, presumably, affected the growth of demand for leisure time.[12]

Yet another way in which leisure time obtained by reducing the work week differs from an ordinary consumer good is that when a worker increases his leisure time he not only loses an hour's wage but also gives up the experience of an hour's work.[13] Hence, when the analysis moves to the discussion of the role played by changes in the relative prices of goods closely related to leisure time (such as commercial recreation), it is also useful to analyze the influence of changes in the relative cost of providing good working conditions on the demand for leisure time.

2.3 THE DEMAND FOR RECREATION AND THE DEMAND FOR LEISURE TIME

The demand for leisure time and the demand for market recreation are closely related. In empirical estimates of the demand for consumer goods it is customary to attempt to isolate the influence of changes in the relative price of closely related goods. This, however, has not been the case in studies of the income-leisure choice. This neglect of the relationship between leisure and recreation has probably been due to the emphasis placed in empirical work on the study of hours of work, as opposed to the analysis of the demand for leisure time.

One of the main purposes of the present work will be to explore this relationship between leisure time and market recreation. The time bud-

12. The effects of these variable returns to hours of work on the demand for leisure time are discussed in sections 2.5-2.11 below.
13. See above, section 1.3.

gets in Table 4-A on pp. 82-83 (as well as the studies cited on pp. 81 and 84) demonstrate that they are, in fact, used together. In that sense, then, leisure and recreation are complements in consumption. But are leisure and recreation complements in the sense that a reduction in the price of one will lead to an increase in the demand for the other? This question is examined directly in Chapter 5 by observing whether a decline in the price of recreation increases the demand for leisure, and conversely, whether a reduction in the price of leisure time increases the demand for recreation.

The relationship between leisure and recreation may also be explored by departing from conventional consumer theory, and using the theory of leisure activities recently developed by Gary Becker.[14] In this analysis a modification of Becker's method is employed which seems more directly helpful in the study of recreation and leisure.

In the activity model, the worker-consumer is regarded as combining consumption time and consumption goods to produce consumption or leisure activities. When the goods are recreational, the resulting activity may be regarded as a 'leisure activity' in the narrower sense of the term.

In this model a leisure activity such as movie-going or card-playing is a function of the inputs used by the consumer (time and goods and services), and of consumer technology, or the way in which the consumer utilizes these resources to create a satisfying activity.

Thus one might write: $A = A(L,R,T)$, where T is a measure of consumer technology. The consumer function A is analogous to the production functions commonly used in the economic analysis of production.

The demand for a leisure activity would be a positive function of real per capita income, and a negative function of the price of the inputs, if the activity is a normal, superior good. Advances in consumer leisure technology might have the same effect on the demand for a leisure activity as do reductions in input prices, that is, they would increase it.

---

14. This discussion of the leisure activity notion was greatly assisted by the reading of an early draft of Gary Becker's 'On the Economics of Time' (paper read before the Econometric Society, Boston, Mass., December 29, 1963). However, the present treatment contains a number of modifications of or departures from Becker's original model, for which changes, of course, he is not responsible. See also his 'A Theory of the Allocation of Time.'

In the leisure activity model, the demand for leisure time and market recreation is derived from the relation of these inputs to the output leisure activity, as well as from the level of the activity itself. For example, a rise in real income might lead first to an increase in the amount of a leisure activity consumed, and hence to an increase in the demand for leisure time and market recreation.

A decline in the relative price of an input would increase the demand for it on two grounds: first, there would be a substitution of this input for the other(s) used in the activity, since it had now become relatively cheaper; and second, the lowered price of the input would lower the relative price of the output, and would thus lead to an expansion of demand for the output and, hence, for the input.

If a price reduction is made in one factor, demand for the other factor(s) will be affected negatively by the substitution effect and positively by the expansion effect. If the second effect dominates, a reduction in the price of one factor will yield an increase in the demand for the other. This is a common definition of complementarity in consumption. If the first effect dominates, the goods are market substitutes.

It is quite possible that one may observe goods and time being consumed simultaneously, yet substitute relationships between them may predominate in the market, rather than complementary relationships. For example, if motion picture admission prices are lowered, an individual may switch from a neighborhood house showing double features to a downtown theater showing first-run single bills. Again, reduced vacation costs would lead some people to trade a month at a nearby seaside resort for three weeks in Europe.[15]

Moreover it would be quite incorrect to use the time intensity of a consumption activity (measured as the ratio of time spent to dollar value of consumption goods used in the activity) as a guide to whether goods and time are complements or substitutes in that activity.[16] Rather, the relevant parameters would be the elasticity of substitution between goods and time in the activity and the price elasticity of demand for the activity.

15. Since 'vacation utility' is produced by varying combinations of vacation time and vacation expenditure.
16. Nor does time intensity help us very much in categorizing activities as leisure or recreational. For some Americans, their daily lunch is a much more 'time-intensive' activity than their regular Saturday night splurge, yet it is the latter that most people would consider to be recreational.

An improvement in consumer technology in utilizing an input should have much the same effect on output as a reduction in the price of the input. But the net effect of the improvement on demand for the input will depend upon the price elasticity for that input (composed of a substitution and an expansion effect) and on the degree of improvement, if any, achieved in the utilization of other inputs.

2.4 WORKING CONDITIONS AND THE DEMAND FOR LEISURE TIME

Market employment provides not only the funds for the worker's consumption but also the experience of working. This experience will be more or less pleasant depending upon the conditions of work.

In the discussion of the work-leisure choice in Chapter 1, it was pointed out that in order to decide whether to increase his leisure time, the rational employee must weigh the utility (or disutility) derived from an extra hour of leisure against the disutility (or utility) derived from an hour of work plus the utility derived from an hour's wage. An obvious conclusion from this analysis is that more pleasant working conditions would be expected, ceteris paribus, to lead to longer hours of work.

But the incorporation of 'working conditions' in a more general analysis of the demand for leisure time is not such a simple matter. Working conditions reflect not only the nature of the work to be performed (a product both of the technology of the industry and the particular capital-labor ratio used in the firm) but also expenditures by employers and employees to make the work experience both more productive and more pleasant. Working conditions themselves are then best treated as endogenous rather than exogenous to the theory of worker-consumer choice.

Further, because working conditions are not bought and sold like typical consumer goods it is not possible to make a simple analogy with market recreation and to analyze the 'market price of working conditions' as a determinant of the work week.

But while employees do not purchase working conditions on the open market in the same way that they purchase, say, water skis, working conditions are established in a market economy, and the relative cost to the employer of providing working conditions may indeed affect both the state of working conditions and the demand for leisure time.

These points can be brought out more clearly with the help of a simple analysis. In the following, all improvements in working conditions are assumed to be made by the employer, and all wages are assumed to be spent off the job. This probably fits the facts fairly well. Although minor improvements in working conditions may be made by employees (who smoke on the job or bring their transistor radios to work), the major changes have, of course, been made by employers.

Let curves A, B, C, and D in Figure 2-A indicate indifference curves of the typical employee for wages and working conditions. Let curves 1, 2, 3, and 4 represent equal expenditure curves for the employer. If one ignores the productive aspects of working conditions, the profit-maximizing employer would be expected to be indifferent among any of the points along one of this set of curves.

FIGURE 2-A

Determination of wages and working conditions

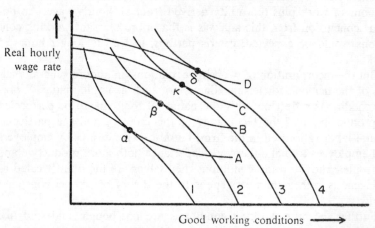

Points α, β, κ, δ represent points of tangency between employer and employee indifference curves, and are then potential positions of equilibrium. At each of these points, the marginal cost to the employer of providing better working conditions is equal to the ratio of the marginal utility of better working conditions to the marginal utility of money to the employee.

The actual choice of one of these potential equilibria (α,β,κ,δ or some similar point) would depend upon the ability of the employees to extract

24

wages from the employer, and thus upon the relative supply and demand of labor.

However, it would be a mistake to assume that this static analysis could be used without modification to explain the improvements over time in working conditions. One could not assume that the expansion path of wages and working conditions that would be followed as the economy progressed would be through α, β, κ, δ. The changes in technology and in the capital-labor ratio that increase the marginal product of, and hence the demand for, labor over time may well affect the relative cost of providing good working conditions, and hence the shape of the curves 1, 2, 3, 4 in Figure 2-A. A workshop, an assembly line, an office, and an automated factory each provides its own special environmental problems.[17]

Or it may be that a 'working conditions industry' is labor-intensive and technically backward, so that it becomes more difficult to provide a given working condition as real wages rise with economic development. For example, the cost of providing an hour of psychological counseling services will rise with the wage rate (although improvements in counseling could offset this to the extent that the cost of *successful* counseling does not rise). Such changes in the relative costs of better working conditions would also affect the shape of curves 1, 2, 3 and 4 in Figure 2-A.

The analysis of working conditions is made much more complicated by the productive consumption effects associated with many improvements in the work environment.[18] Many, perhaps most, employer expenditures on working conditions make a positive contribution to the output of the worker, as well as making his work more pleasant. Improvements in lighting, heating, and ventilation would all fall into this category. But not all employer expenditures on working conditions reflect a coincidence of employer and employee interests. For example, the employer may find that the rhythms of semiclassical music are most suited to the work pace in his factory. Yet he may be forced to pipe in rock and roll in order to satisfy a youthful work force. Alternatively, he may introduce a new work routine, to which his employees are pas-

17. Moreover, different types of work produce different types of people. The tastes of office workers are likely to be different in a number of ways from those of coal miners.
18. Cf. the discussion of the effects on the work-leisure choice of productive consumption in the more traditional sense in section 2.7 below. Note that working conditions are received per hour of work, so that no economies (or diseconomies) of scale are associated with longer hours of work here.

sionately opposed, in the interests of managerial efficiency. As Figure 2-B shows, a variety of possibilities present themselves.

When the effects of working conditions on production are taken into account, the equilibrium solution for the profit-maximizing entrepreneur will continue to require that net marginal cost of improving working conditions be equal to the employee's tradeoff between wages and working conditions, equal in turn, as before, to the ratio of the marginal utility of better working conditions to the marginal utility of money to the employee. But this net marginal cost will now be equal to the difference between the gross marginal cost of improving working conditions and the savings (or dissavings) accruing to the entrepreneur from the increase (or decrease) in product arising out of the employer expenditure on working conditions.[19]

FIGURE 2-B
Working conditions, output, and employee preferences

Employer expenditures on working conditions
Effect on output

		+	−	0
	+	Lighting, heating	Rock and roll music	Picture on the wall
Employee preference	−	Tighter work schedules		
	0	New desk arrangement		

Changes in working conditions with economic development
Effect on output

		+	−	0
	+	+	?	+
Employee preference	−	?		
	0	+		

19. If we let $MP_{L,WC}$ = marginal product of working conditions, then this equilibrium condition can be written as: Net MC_{WC} = Gross MC_{WC} − $MRP_{L,WC}$ = $-\dfrac{dW}{dWC}$ $(= U_{WC}/U_M)$.

26

Thus the net marginal cost will be less than the gross marginal cost only if the expenditure tended to increase output. If the expenditure were for a change that the workers did not want, the net marginal cost should, in equilibrium, be negative.

The introduction of a relationship between working conditions and production will also complicate the dynamic analysis of the changes in working conditions brought about by economic development.

When capital investment or technical change raises the level of wages in the economy, increased labor productivity is usually accompanied by increases in the absolute value of the marginal product of improved working conditions. The simplest example of this would be a case in which the working condition tended, under both the new and the old technology, to make the worker produce one per cent more rapidly per X dollars of expenditures. Then, if wages doubled, the marginal product of improved working conditions would also double. Alternatively, the new technology might lead to a greater or smaller percentage payoff per X dollar of expenditure.

These positive production incentives might cooperate with a favorable reception of the change by the workers to yield much more of it with economic progress (e.g., lighting, heating, ventilation).

But if workers did not like a working condition that contributed to output (for example, the use of recorded music to speed output), they might use the better market for labor to insist on its curtailment, rather than permit its expansion. In other words, if economic development raises the ability of the worker to obtain better terms from the employer, the worker may choose to take part of the improvement in better working conditions for himself, *even if the cost of his choice rises at the same rate as his hourly wage.* If the cost of a working condition rises more rapidly than the wage rate, its improvement is less likely, but still not impossible.

Similarly, working conditions which are preferred by the worker but which are counterproductive become more costly as the economy progresses. However, unless they become *relatively* more costly, it is quite likely that such practices will spread.

There is of course an analogy in these last two categories of working conditions with the income-leisure choice itself. Since economic progress raises the cost of these better working conditions, while at the same time it expands the overall consumption horizons of the worker, it creates a negative substitution effect and a positive income effect. It is thus not clear whether under these circumstances the rational employee will choose better or worse working conditions.

Finally, it should be pointed out that working conditions will be affected not only by employer expenditures, but by the extent to which leisure is taken on the job. Coffee or smoke breaks, or perhaps a general slowing down of the work pace, are ways of taking it easy that may compete with the shorter work day in providing more leisure time. Since time spent in market employment is, for simplicity, classified as work time in this study, coffee breaks and speedups would come under the heading of changes in working conditions whose cost to the employer is simply a loss of output.[20] Again, economic development would be expected to produce a positive income effect tending to encourage, e.g., coffee breaks, along with a negative substitution effect which might discourage such on-the-job leisure.

When one examines the actual conditions of work in the United States in the last sixty years, it is obvious, first, that there has been a net improvement. However, two related questions, which are crucial to understanding the relationship between working conditions and the income-leisure choice, must go unanswered until further empirical work is done. First, what is the cause of these improvements in working conditions? Have they come about because of (or despite) their productive consumption aspects; because of shifts in the occupational mix or other changes induced by changing technology; or simply because of increased demand for better working conditions as a result of higher per capita real income? Second, have conditions of work time improved more rapidly than conditions of consumption time, so that, as a result, work is less unattractive relative to leisure than it once was?

It is obvious that the improvements in working conditions that have taken place have slowed the pace of hours reduction below that which would have held if 1900 conditions of work had been maintained. However, an empirical study of some of the more interesting issues raised here, such as the economic analysis of the causes of observed improvements in working conditions, or the effects of changes in working conditions on changes in the demand for leisure time, must be delayed until more of the relevant data are available.

20. Which might be less than proportionate to the time taken off if the worker is refreshed, more than proportionate if his break disorganizes the work of others (e.g., if the secretaries take coffee breaks and the executives do not, or vice versa).

2.5 VARIABLE RETURNS TO HOURS OF WORK: A STATEMENT OF THE PROBLEM

The traditional analysis of the income-leisure choice as a function of the real wage rate implicitly assumes that employees may increase or reduce their hours of work without affecting their average hourly earnings, but this assumption is contradicted in a number of important ways. In practice, variable rather than constant returns to hours of work prevail.

Income-leisure opportunity curves showing increasing, constant, and decreasing returns to hours of work are presented as curves 1, 2, and 3, respectively, of Figure 2-C below.

FIGURE 2-C
Variable returns to hours of work

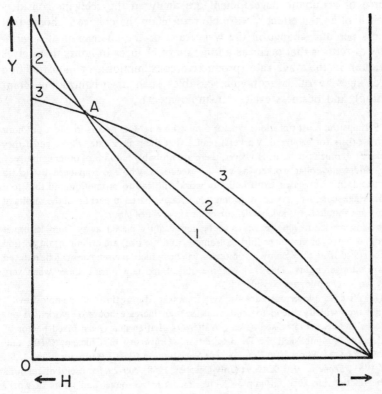

Clearly, economic theory would predict that if an individual faces curve 2, the case in which income is proportionate to hours worked, and picks point A, then: (a) when offered curve 1 (increasing returns) he will work the same or longer hours; and (b) when offered curve 3 (decreasing returns) he will work the same or fewer hours than indicated by position A.

Examples of these variable returns to hours of work are plentiful. The biases in the income-leisure choice created by fatigue, productive consumption, education, commuting, government finance, and unemployment are described in the following pages. Many other potentially significant cases of variable returns to hours of work might be identified.[21]

However, for some purposes it is not sufficient simply to identify a bias and to point out the probable direction of its effect on the income-leisure choice. When changes in the demand for leisure time in the course of economic development are analyzed the relevant consideration is often the effect of variable returns on the change in hours that results per unit change in the wage rate, or the changes in the *variability* of returns that occur as a function of changes in hours themselves (fatigue), in the wage rate (productive consumption), or as a function of changes in other economic variables such as urbanization (commuting), and business cycles (unemployment).

21. Perhaps the most notorious type of diminishing returns occurs in effort per hour when workers (or groups of workers) realize that their piece rate will be cut if they produce too much per hour. However, there are probably millions of other employees, blue- and white-collar workers as well as executives, who are convinced that extra effort and, in many cases, extra hours of work will lead to promotion and thus to a higher wage scale. Any system of promotion which is based in part upon the results of hard work should bias the labor-leisure choice in favor of labor.

The income-leisure choice will also be significantly biased away from leisure if personnel costs per employee (hiring, training, and the like) are an important portion of labor cost. If so, the employer's unit costs will be reduced if employees can be induced to work longer hours. This may become quite important during times when very short work schedules are considered.

(These fixed employee costs are also very important during times of unemployment – though they will then tend to reduce rather than increase hours of work [see pp. 52-56 below].) See FINEGAN, *op cit.*; Walter OI, 'Labor as a Quasi-Fixed Factor of Production' (unpublished Ph.D. dissertation, University of Chicago, 1960); and Sherwin ROSEN, 'Short-Run Employment Variation on Class-I Railroads in the U.S., 1947-1963', *Econometrica*, XXXVI (July-October, 1968), 511-29, for useful discussions of the relationship between employer investments in personnel and hours of work.

For example, the variability of returns brought about by fatigue will vanish if hours of work are shortened sufficiently.

Variable returns to hours of work also create some interesting measurement problems in the empirical analysis of the income-leisure decision. If there are constant returns (and if property income is negligible), differences in the real wage rate, measured as average hourly earnings, may approximate relative differences in real income or in the price of leisure.[22] But under a system of variable returns this three-way correspondence breaks down. In general, one finds that when fatigue or productive consumption is important, the conventional measure of the real hourly wage rate is a good index of income but a poor measure of the price of leisure. Just the reverse is true when education predominates.

The conceptual and measurement problems of time series analysis of the demand for leisure time under conditions of variable returns will be discussed in the remaining sections of this chapter.

2.6 OUTPUT-REDUCING FATIGUE AND THE DEMAND FOR LEISURE TIME

Variable returns to hours of work are important both in a subsistence or quasi-subsistence economy and under more prosperous conditions. However, the forces creating these variable returns, and hence the function relating income to effort, will be quite different. These differences are important in the determination of the demand for leisure time, and hence it is important to emphasize that from 1900 to 1960 the United States labor force underwent a transition from a period in which a large portion of employees might be described as at a quasi-subsistence level [23] both in consumption goods and services and in consumption time to a period in which economic development had almost totally changed the condition of most workers to one of relative affluence.

Thus, the effects of fatigue were far more important in the determination of the demand for leisure in the period before 1929 than they have been since. Hours of work fell sharply during the depression of

22. But see below, Chapter 5, for an attempt to improve upon the conventional measure by including leisure time in real income, and the price of leisure in the price deflator used to obtain both the relative price of leisure and real income.
23. See below, p. 39.

the nineteen thirties and never again rose (at least in peacetime) to a level at which output-reducing fatigue could become important for the average worker.

However, if one wants to use the record of the past sixty years to give some insight into the process of leisure determination in the United States, it is necessary to understand the role played by fatigue, and especially, by the transition from a fatigue to a non-fatigue equilibrium.

The phenomenon of fatigue affects the demand for leisure in two ways. First, as hours are lengthened and fatigue sets in, work becomes increasingly onerous. This discomfort (combined with the inconvenience of having too little time for the usual consumption pursuits and the relative satisfaction of the need for money income) would limit hours of work even if the employee were permitted by his employer to work as many hours as he wished at the going wage rate. If one thinks of the demand for leisure time per worker as a function of income and of the market tradeoff between income and hours of work, then this discomfort effect of fatigue may be regarded as influencing the parameters of the demand function.

But of course fatigue also affects the income level and the market tradeoff between income and hours of work themselves (i.e., the price of leisure). The profit-maximizing employer cannot be expected to pay the same wage per hour for long hours of work if fatigue is reducing productivity per hour.

It is this relationship of fatigue to output that is most readily susceptible to economic analysis.[24]

A large body of evidence has been collected on the effect of hours of work on output.[25] The hours-output relationship has been shown to vary from task to task and from worker to worker. Moreover, quanti-

24. But the effects of the discomforts of fatigue on consumer choice can be measured statistically by observing the parameters of the demand for leisure function when hours of work are long. One should remember, however, that long hours schedules are usually accompanied by low income. Hence, the worker's fatigue discomfort may well be offset in the demand function by the discomfort of hunger and other physical wants, which increase with shorter hours.

25. For a brief summary of such studies, see Herbert R. NORTHRUP and Herbert R. BRINBERG, *Economics of the Workweek* (National Industrial Conference Board Studies in Business Economics, No. 24; New York: National Industrial Conference Board, 1950). See also the more recent discussion of these studies in Irving F. LEVESON, 'Reductions in Hours of Work as a Source of Productivity Growth', *Journal of Political Economy*, LXXII, No. 2 (April, 1967), 199-204.

tative results will be affected by the method used by the investigator in dealing with quality of output, evaluation of accidents, the relationship between absenteeism and the wage rate at a given level of hours, the long-term effects of hours of work on the worker's productivity, and the like.[26]

However, most investigators agree that in the range from 0 to about 40-48 hours a week, an additional hour of work contributes to 'output' an amount not less than that contributed by the average of hours up to this point; that as hours rise from 40-48 to some level between 60 and 120, output rises with hours, but at a decreasing rate, i.e., each successive hour makes a smaller contribution to output; and, finally, that an entrepreneur foolish enough to schedule hours per week at a level above the 60-120 range would find that total output was declining as hours rose.

In 1900, the weekly hours schedules of the great majority of employees were in the 48-84 hours range. In any event, most schedules lay well within the range 40-48 to 60-120, i.e., at levels where output rises with hours of work, but at a decreasing rate, so that the price of leisure would be greater than zero but less than the base or fatigueless wage. This 'fatigue factor' presumably declined in importance after 1900, as hours declined. According to one group of analysts,[27] by 1950, when hours had been reduced to the 0 to 40-48 range, the 'fatigue factor' had ceased to be relevant to American conditions. They argued that any further reduction in hours would yield a reduction in output fully proportional to the cut in hours.

Thus, the period 1900 to 1960 in the United States encompasses a transition from an era of fatigue to one of non-fatigue (in the output-reducing sense), or from what one might term a state of quasi-subsistence to one of relative affluence in consumption time. Figure 2-D shows how a typical worker might pass from fatigue to non-fatigue conditions as he moves from A to B to C.[28] This transition would undoubtedly affect the demand for leisure time. Analysis of this change also raises at least four questions: 1. What effect did fatigue have on hours of work? 2. What effect did fatigue have on the responsiveness

26. Some additional measurement problems are introduced in the section on productive consumption below.
27. NORTHRUP and BRINBERG, *Economics of the Workweek*.
28. A basic assumption in this diagram and in the following exposition is that the worker is paid according to some measure of his productivity.

of hours of work to changes in the wage rate? 3. What distortions would be introduced into the analysis of the level of hours of work if

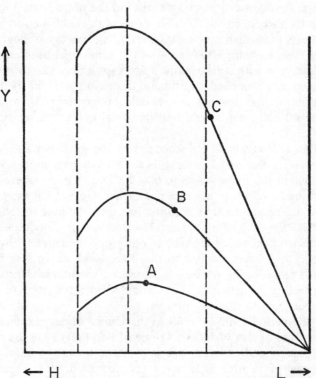

FIGURE 2-D
Output-reducing fatigue and hours of work

we used average hourly earnings as a proxy for the base (i.e., fatigue-less) wage rate and for the price of leisure? 4. What distortions would be introduced into the rate of change of hours of work by the method used in 3?

These questions are best answered separately:

1. The introduction of fatigue reduces the price of an hour of work (the price of leisure) at any level of hours above that at which fatigue takes place. Money income would also be reduced, though by a much smaller percentage. Since it is generally thought that the income elasti-

city of leisure is greater than its price elasticity, **the effect of output-** reducing fatigue on hours is indeterminate.

The net outcome would depend on the form of the fatigue function (the function that relates income to hours of work under conditions of fatigue) as well as on that of the leisure demand function. For example, it seems obvious that a fatigue function of Type A in the table below is more likely to yield a reduction in hours than the (less typical) function in Type B. Experiments were also made with conventional 'constant elasticity' demand relations. From these (see Mathematical Note 2-A in the Appendix for two examples of them), it would seem that the income effect would have to be quite large relative to the price effect for hours to be *lengthened* by the introduction of fatigue.

Labor output = Labor income

Hours	No fatigue	Type A fatigue	Type B fatigue
1	1	1	1
2	2	2	1.5
40	40	40	20
45	45	43	22
50	50	45	24

2. The response of hours of work to changes in the base wage rate is also affected by the introduction of fatigue. When hours are reduced in response to a rise in the base wage rate, the price of leisure rises as a result both of the increase in the wage rate and of the reduction in hours (due to the diminution of the fatigue effect). That is, the price of leisure will rise at a rate that is more than proportionate to the wage rate. In itself, this will produce a smaller change in hours in response to a given change in the wage rate than would prevail in the absence of fatigue. Income also rises at a rate that is more than proportionate to the wage rate, but the effect here is much smaller.

Again, experimentation with constant elasticity models (see Mathematical Note 2-A) leads one to guess that unless the income effect is quite large relative to the substitution effect, the elasticity of hours with respect to the base wage rate is reduced, not increased, by the introduction of the fatigue factor.

35

3. If fatigue conditions exist, average hourly earnings will underestimate the base or fatigueless wage and will overestimate the price of leisure.[29]

Under fatigue conditions the use of average hourly earnings in place of the base wage will lead one (if lower wages produce longer hours) to expect workers' hours to be longer than they, in fact, are.

4. This measurement error will also lead to an overestimate of the relative change in hours with respect to a given change in the observed wage rate. This distortion results from the fact that average hourly earnings will rise more than in proportion to the wage rate as hours decline. Thus the increase in wages, and hence the change in hours, is overestimated.

When one turns from the abstract analysis of the effects of fatigue to the time series data, it becomes clear that two periods are being compared: an earlier period in which hours of work are determined under fatigue conditions, and in which the conventional measure of wage rates (average hourly earnings) is an underestimate of the base (or fatigueless) wage, and a later period, where fatigue is not a problem and where the base wage is measured more or less corectly by the average hourly earnings.

This observation raises two additional questions: what is the combined, net effect of these two forces (output-reducing fatigue, and the measurement error produced by output-reducing fatigue) on (5) the relationship between the observed wage rate and hours and (6) the rate of change in hours with respect to a change in the observed wage rate?

5. If average hourly earnings are used as a proxy for the base wage and no fatigue effect is assumed where it in fact exists, money income and leisure will be measured correctly but the price of leisure will be overestimated. Thus, hours of work would be estimated as longer than they in fact are. (In our constant elasticity models, hours worked were reduced here regardless of the relative sizes of the income and substitution effects.)

6. The biases introduced into the empirical analysis of the relation between changes in the wage rate and changes in hours of work by ignoring the effects of fatigue on the price of leisure and by using

29. As long as the elasticity of labor income with respect to hours of work is less than 1.

36

average hourly earnings as a proxy for the base wage also operate unambiguously. The measurement of changes in money income and in leisure will be correct, but measurements of increases in average hourly earnings will underestimate the true change in the price of leisure. Thus a greater decline in hours of work would be expected than actually takes place. (In the constant elasticity models examined, this result held true regardless of the size of the parameters of the demand function.)

An important result of this last conclusion for empirical work is that one would expect an acceleration in the rate of change in hours of work with respect to a given change in the observed 'wage rate' as the economy moves from the fatigue to the non-fatigue period.

2.7 PRODUCTIVE CONSUMPTION AND THE DEMAND FOR LEISURE TIME

Just as fatigue (which might be regarded as productive consumption in time) produces diminishing returns to hours of work for the employee, productive consumption in goods and services under conditions of quasi-subsistence will yield increasing returns to hours of work. Productive consumption may be said to exist when higher income levels, which permit the worker to enjoy a higher standard of living, enable him to perform with greater vigor at his work. Longer hours under these conditions will lead to higher income and hence to better health and greater energy. Better physical fitness will in turn lead to higher average hourly earnings.

Productive consumption, in this strict sense, is probably not very important for the average American worker of today. However, there is considerable evidence that consumption and productivity were causally related in the United States in 1900 and in the early decades of this century. Thus, the first sixty years of this century were marked by the disappearance of productive consumption as an important phenomenon. In this respect, there is again an obvious parallel with output-reducing fatigue.

But the impact of productive consumption on the income-leisure choice can be seen most clearly by abstracting from the fatigue effect, and considering a group of workers whose productivity is simply increased by their consumption.

In this case, income will rise at an increasing rate as hours of work are prolonged.[30] Figure 2-E shows the income-leisure opportunities open to a worker faced with productive consumption in goods (the fatigue effect is omitted). It would seem that the worker would put in more hours here than he would if he earned his average hourly earnings at all levels of hours. It is not clear that the worker would work more hours if he had the same piece rate but maintained his bodily

FIGURE 2-E

Productive consumption and the demand for leisure time

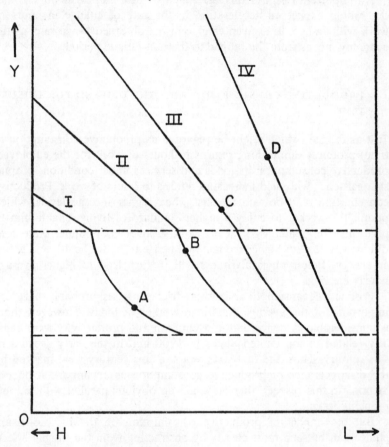

30. Let the workers be paid at a piece rate P. Let daily output equal O, hourly output equal O*. Then $O = HO^*(PO)$, and $\dfrac{dPO}{dH} = \dfrac{PO^*}{1 - PHO^*_{PO}} > PO^*.$

38

strength from other sources (e.g., a relative or a pension). Moreover, when one turns to the set of curves I, II, III, and IV, which show the income-leisure opportunity sets corresponding to various levels of piece rates,[31] one sees that the analysis of the effects of productive consumption on the rate of change of hours of work with respect to changes in the piece rate is quite complicated.

However, a simple empirical use of productive consumption may be made by combining it with the fatigue effect. One might analyze the two simultaneously by considering the worker's output to be some general function of his income and of his hours of work. The tradeoff between income and work then will be simultaneously increased by the productive consumption effect and decreased by the fatigue effect.[32] The two effects will cancel each other so that the elasticity of income with respect to work time will be equal to unity only if the *sum* of the elasticity of output with respect to work (consumption held constant) and of output with respect to consumption were equal to unity. Under those circumstances, the worker's income would be in proportion to his hours of work.

An attempt is made in Figure 2-F to show some ways in which the fatigue and productive consumption arguments might combine. Income levels below A are not sufficient to sustain life. Between A and B productive consumption effects take place. This is the region of 'quasi-subsistence' in consumption. Increases in income above level B do not provide higher output. On the time axis a consumption time level of C is necessary to sustain life. Increases in leisure time (reductions in work time) from C to E yield higher average hourly earnings, so that the worker in this region might be said to be at the 'quasi-subsistence' level of consumption time. Hours of work less than E do not increase average hourly earnings. Output is maximized at the D level of hours.

Since one would not expect the typical worker in a market society to put in more than D hours, and since A represents the subsistence consumption level, workers would be expected to be found only in the region to the right of D and above A. This region might then be subdivided into four quadrants: I, no productive consumption or fatigue effect; II, fatigue effect but no productive consumption effect; III, pro-

31. Note that when faced with curves III and IV the worker, by choosing points C and D, respectively, raises himself above that level of money income where productive consumption would be relevant.

32. Mathematically, if $O = O(H, PO)$, then $\dfrac{dPO}{dH} = \dfrac{PO_H}{1 - PO_{PO}}$.

FIGURE 2-F
Subsistence in consumption goods and consumption time

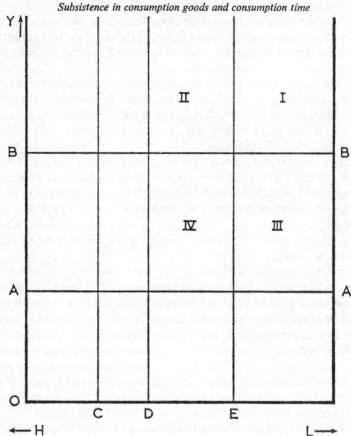

ductive consumption effect, but no fatigue effect; and IV, both fatigue and productive consumption effects.

Thus constant returns to hours of work prevail in quadrant I, increasing returns in quadrant II, and decreasing returns in quadrant III. It is not clear which will predominate in quadrant IV. For example, in the notation used in Footnote 30, p. 38, if $O = 8(H)^{3/4}(PO)^{1/4}$ the worker is in quadrant IV, with both the fatigue and productive consumption effects operative. But since this is the case where the sum of the elasticities equals unity the fatigue effect just cancels the productive consumption effect, and constant returns to hours of work prevail: $O = 16H(P)^{4/3}$. In this respect, quadrant IV is most like quadrant I.

A given group of workers might face an opportunity line extending through several of these quadrants,[33] although the point on the line chosen by a worker would, of course, be found in only one quadrant.[34]

This analysis of productive consumption is interesting in itself, but it also has some practical relevance for the empirical analyses of hours of work, especially where workers are in quadrant IV (quasi-subsistence in both time and goods). If one wants to measure the effect of hours of work on output so that one can capture both the fatigue and the productive consumption effects as they influenced the historical course of hours reduction (obtaining what will be called in this discussion the 'net fatigue effect'), rather than the fatigue effect in isolation (what will be called the 'gross fatigue effect'), then one would prefer to use data contemporary with the period in which fatigue predominated and in which hours and wages were set in the market. Thus, one should distrust any experimental data in which the employer changed hours but kept income constant. Such an experiment might yield an apparent fatigue effect where no *net* fatigue existed.

By the same token, one must be very cautious in using the output-hours data from World War II (in some ways the best available data on fatigue). In this extraordinary period, some defense workers were well above the subsistence level in food, clothing, and the like, but quite close to the subsistence level in sleep, recreation, and free time generally. The output-hours relation observed under these conditions would probably show a greater net fatigue effect than that which actually prevailed at lower wage rates.[35] In other words, it is likely that

33. The logical possibilities are: III; III and II; IV and III; IV, III, and II; IV and II; and IV, I, and II.

34. This exposition abstracts from a number of issues that might be of importance in empirical work. For example, interrelationships among the productive consumption effect and fatigue effect might exist, so that the level of hours (E) that maximizes output may be either a rising or a declining function of productive consumption (e.g., underfed or sickly workers might produce more by working long hours at a slow pace).

Moreover, the system of curves would be affected by the way in which workers chose to spend their time and money. Some workers on low piece rates *did* spend their limited time and money on boozing, gambling, or eating fish and chips or sweets and the like. In this respect the American slave south (where worker consumption was controlled by the master) would probably provide an interesting contrast with worker consumption in the free sections of the country in the early nineteenth century.

35. In particular, one is more reluctant to accept the view that entrepreneurs and employees were irrational in the nineteenth century when they scheduled hours of work that seem excessive in the light of the results of modern fatigue studies.

if one were to apply output-hours parameters derived from World War II or from experimental conditions, rather than from contemporary market data, one would be overestimating the empirical importance of the effects on hours of work of the transition from a period of (output-reducing) fatigue to a period of non- (output-reducing) fatigue.

Output-reducing fatigue and productive consumption of the usual sort are quite relevant to the study of an industrial society at a stage of development where the bulk of its work force is at or near the subsistence level. In our more affluent society, with its higher wage rates, these problems have largely been eliminated. In terms of his physical capacities, the average worker is in quadrant I of Figure 2-F, where increases in output are proportionate to increases in hours of work. However, it is not true that, with advanced economic development, economies or diseconomies of scale in hours of work have disappeared. On the contrary, not only have some of the factors producing variable returns continued to operate, but a number of new ones have been created by economic development. Under the heading of long-standing causes of variable returns to work, one might cite unemployment in the labor market.

But it may also be argued that economic development has given rise to economies of scale to hours of effort through the spread of educational opportunities and through the development of attractive commuting possibilities. Moreover, the development of a complicated system of government finance, especially the progressive income tax, undoubtedly produces variable returns to work for most people.

2.8 EDUCATION AND THE DEMAND FOR LEISURE TIME

One of the more important results of economic development in the United States in the past sixty years has been an increase in the level of education of the average employee. The great proliferation of educational opportunities in these years has tended to create economies of scale in work time, thus tending to discourage the demand for leisure time.

If it is assumed that the average individual has the same working hours throughout his productive years, it is easy to compare lifetime income and lifetime leisure. If one first assumes a zero rate of time discount, and no tuition charges, then the average annual labor income of the individual in

his productive years will be (1) $Y = \dfrac{W(HP - S)}{P}$, where W (hourly wage

42

rate) is a function of S (total study time), P is years of work and study, and H is hours of work or study per year. The tradeoff on the margin between income and hours of work will be equal to W, the wage rate.[36] But the wage rate, W, is greater than the average return to effort, (2) $Y/H = W - S/PH$. Thus, increasing returns to effort are present here.

In equilibrium, it can be shown that (3) $E_{Y,H} = 1 + E_{W,S}$ (if optimal S is chosen). This result (3) is also obtained if time preference is introduced and the individual is permitted to borrow against his future earnings at a (fixed) rate of interest so as to obtain an equal flow of money income over his productive years.[37] (See Mathematical Note 2-B for a demonstration of these points.) Moreover, the elasticity of income with respect to hours will continue to be greater than 1 (indicating increasing returns to hours of effort) if one permits a fixed tuition charge per unit of study time (with either the zero or the positive discount rate variant), although equation (3) will no longer hold.

The analysis of the income-leisure choice will be further complicated if the wage structure itself is changed because a sector of the labor force takes advantage of the new educational opportunities. However, it can be shown that while an increase in the proportion of the labor force with a high level of education may tend to lower the wages of the well educated relative to those of the less well educated, it will not eliminate the economies of scale in hours of work.

If all workers were identical in tastes and in resources, the opportunity line relating the discounted value of income and leisure would represent an indifference schedule for those levels chosen (other combinations, available but not chosen, would, of course, lie on inferior indifference curves). This schedule would lie on an indifference curve which would be intermediate between the original position and that chosen when education first became available.

If workers had different tastes, the resulting opportunity curve need not be anybody's indifference curve. However, there would still be economies of scale in work as long as the work requiring more education paid a higher hourly wage rate to compensate for the years of (unpaid) study. As long as this condition is met, the elasticity of income with respect to hours of effort is greater than 1. These increasing returns might produce a tendency towards longer hours of work. Figure

36. See Mathematical Note 2-B in the Appendix.
37. The introduction of a constant productivity improvement factor will have the same effect as a reduction in the rate of interest.

2-G-1 illustrates the case where interest rates are equal to zero. Figure 2-G-2 shows a positive interest rate. In each figure the heavy lines show those opportunities that might be chosen.

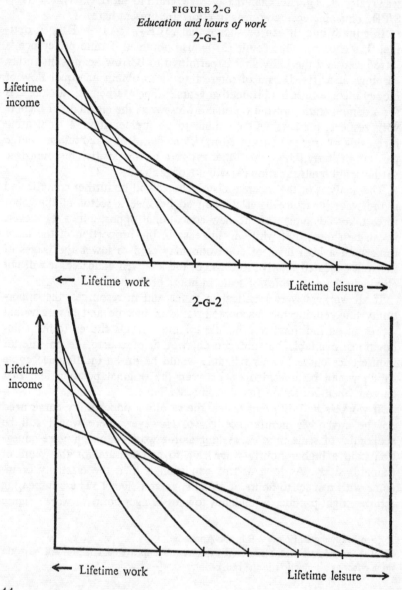

FIGURE 2-G
Education and hours of work
2-G-1

Lifetime income

← Lifetime work   Lifetime leisure →

2-G-2

Lifetime income

← Lifetime work   Lifetime leisure →

*Problems of Utilizing Education in an Empirical Analysis of the Demand for
Leisure Time*

Leisure time, average hourly earnings, and education itself are endogenous in this model, i.e., they are determined within the system. The
exogenous education variable which would help to determine the endogenous variables might be called 'proliferation of educational opportunities.' But it is difficult to identify this opportunity variable or to
measure it empirically.[38]

However, one can at least speculate on the probable effects that increased educational opportunities have had on the demand for leisure
time. If the level of education in the labor force in the twentieth century in the United States is examined, one sees that it is not only rising,
but that it *seems* to be rising at an increasing rate (the data are too in-
conclusive to make any stronger statement). At the same time, hours
of work have been falling at a decreasing rate, both with respect to
time and with respect to the wage rate. It is plausible then that the
proliferation of educational opportunities has contributed to a slowdown in the rate of growth in the demand for leisure time.

38. For example, in the models of leisure and education presented here, there is no
positive line of causation from the wage level to education, unless tuition is charged.
Even if tuition is charged, one can only be certain that a rise in the wage rate will yield
an increase in years of schooling if the rather artificial assumption is retained that there
is only one possible quality of education. If one permits this hypothetical student to
pay higher tuition and, by thus substituting other resources for his time, to achieve
more rapid educational progress, one cannot tell whether a rise in the wage rate will
lead to a larger or smaller total of student time expended. (Nor could one predict the
effect on study time of a reduction in tuition charges.) The outcome would depend upon
the elasticity of substitution between student time and other educational resources, as
well as on the increase in educational level.

   In fact, there may well be a line of causation from higher wages to lower time preferences, or rates of discounting the future, and thence to higher educational levels.
This is a fairly common argument, and one that seems to fit the facts. In addition, there
is the similarly plausible argument, made by G.S. Becker (G.S. BECKER, *Human
Capital* (N.Y.: Columbia University Press, 1964), Footnote 27 on page 53), that increases in education have been produced in part by technological changes in education that have increased its payoff function. Changes in life expectancy, greater
subsidies to the public school system, dynamic propagation mechanisms (education
of children in one generation leading to educated parents in the next, and thence to a
higher level of educational aspiration for their children) may all have played a role
in the raising of the educational level.

Education and the Measurement of Income

If the labor force is characterized by a high educational level, then average hourly earnings may overestimate income. Moreover, if the level of education of the labor force increases, the resulting improvement in hourly earnings may overestimate the true gain in income. These overestimates of income will in turn bias estimates of the income-leisure choice.[39]

Such measurement problems will arise if one wishes to measure income over the worker's economically productive lifetime (say, from age six to age sixty-five). Since a proportion of these years are spent in school, the uncritical use of average hourly earnings data as a measure of income will of course overestimate the desired estimate of average income. Similarly, if the educational level is rising, the percentage increase in average hourly earnings will be greater than that in lifetime income.

However, changes in the educational level will not distort the measurement of the price of leisure. Hence, if lifetime rather than current income is the correct determinant of the income-leisure choice, then this overestimate of the rate of growth of income (accompanied by a correct measurement of the price of leisure) would predict a greater increase in the demand for leisure time than would actually occur.

Other Effects of Education on the Demand for Leisure Time

The increased level of education of the labor force will have effects on the demand for leisure apart from those operating through changes in real income and the price of leisure.

First, the level of education will affect the desirability of work. The study of a profession for some years, and then the practice of it for the rest of one's life may each be more or less pleasant activities than spending the same years at the kind of job typically held by the less well educated. Insofar as such work is preferred, one might expect less of an aversion to work, and hence longer hours of work, from the better educated.

Second, education is supposed to improve the ability of the student to enjoy consumption experiences, as well as to enable him to earn a

39. Estimates of the demand for consumer goods will be affected in the same way by this underestimate of income.

46

better living. It has often been stated that the individual will be inclined towards shorter hours as he learns to utilize his leisure.

But this is an oversimplified view of human behavior. While it may be empirically true that those who know how to use their leisure will want more of it, it is at least possible that some will therefore need less of it; e.g., it would take a well-educated person little time to read the tabloid that the less well-educated citizen pores over.[40]

Moreover, through education one learns to utilize consumer goods as well as time in the consumption experience. Again, this knowledge will lead to an ability to conserve consumer goods, but it will also lead to an expansion in the level of consumption activity. For example, a knowledge of automobiles and of aesthetics may lead one to reject the conventional tail-finned monster. But will the connoisseur purchase a VW beetle, or will he strive for a Mercedes-Benz?

Thus, it is difficult to see why, on *a priori* grounds, education in consumption will lead one to a choice of more time-intensive consumption activities.

On balance, then, the consideration of these two additional relationships (better working conditions and more intelligent consumption) between education and the demand for leisure time would seem to lend further support to the view that there would be a negative relationship between education and the demand for leisure time.

2.9 COMMUTING AND LEISURE TIME

An important result of economic development, and especially of urbanization, in the United States is that a large percentage of all employees now travel long distances each day to and from work, using up anywhere from one to three or more hours per day. This activity is not only an important user of time but also one which may give rise to economies of scale in the work day. Hence, it may tend to increase the length of the effective work day and thus reduce the demand for leisure time.

One way to analyze commuting activity is to regard the worker's residence as fixed and his daily travel trip as a method of finding better-paying work. Alternatively, one might regard his place of work as fixed, and his commuting as an effort to obtain lower prices for a num-

40. See discussion of consumer technology on pp. 21-23.)

ber of items in his budget, especially housing, schools, and recreation,[41] and thus to raise his real wage rate. For analytical simplicity, in what follows commuting will be considered to be wage-increasing.

Suppose that there exist a number of jobs at varying distances from the worker's home, which are equally satisfying to him in terms of the income and leisure they offer. For this condition to be satisfied, the jobs further from home must pay higher hourly wage rates, since they require commuting time and fares. Then, assuming convex indifference curves of the usual sort, equilibrium at the jobs further from home will require less leisure per day and more money income than those closer to home.

Even if the worker-commuter is not confronted with a range of equally attractive commuting possibilities, it can be deduced that the elasticity of his income with respect to his hours of work plus travel is greater than 1 at his present place of work. (His wage rate will be greater than his average hourly earnings if travel time is included in the hours base.) These economies of scale in work may induce him to take less leisure than if he were a non-commuter.

However, if the wage rate rises rapidly enough with time traveled,[42] it is possible that hours of paid work are fewer further from home. Thus, one would expect commuters to have less leisure but would not necessarily expect them to have longer hours of paid work.

The equilibrium conditions for commuters who are maximizing their utility at a given level of leisure time are given in Mathematical Note 2-C in the Appendix.[43]

---

41. This is certainly the correct model to use in the analysis of shopping trips. See George J. STIGLER, 'The Economics of Information', *Journal of Political Economy*, LXIX (June, 1961), 213-25. See John D. OWEN, 'The Value of Commuter Speed', *Western Economic Journal*, VII (June, 1969), 164-72, for a model in which price reductions as well as wage increases are considered; see also the useful discussions of commuter time in G. S. BECKER, 'A Theory of the Allocation of Time', and Jacob MINCER, 'Market Prices, Opportunity Costs, and Income Effects', in Carl CHRIST, ed., *Measurement in Economics* (Stanford, Calif.: Stanford University Press, 1963).

42. Holding speed constant, it is only necessary that $E_{W_T,T} > E_{W,T} \left(\dfrac{WT}{WT + F} \right)$, where W = hourly wage, T = travel time, and F = travel fare. See BECKER, 'A Theory of the Allocation of Time', p. 512, for a somewhat different formulation.

43. The individual is assumed there to be indifferent in the choice between travel and work time. A more general model is developed in OWEN, 'The Value of Commuter Speed'.

Parallels Between Commuting and Education

The careful reader will see that the model here is conceptually identical with the education model with zero rate of interest (level of education is equated with distance traveled; tuition is equated with fare; time spent in education is equated with time spent in travel). Once again, the worker's time is being spent in a non-market activity which will serve to raise his hourly wage rate when he does arrive at his market employment. The one difference between the two models is that fare per hour has been permitted to vary with speed in the mathematical note, while in the discussion of education variable tuition was discussed only in the text.

Another parallel between commuting and education may be found if commuting is considered to be price-reducing as well as wage-increasing. If commuting produces a change in the consumption environment, then it may tend to induce a change in the goods-time mix in consumption. This analysis is similar to that of 'education for consumption' and, again, it is difficult to say whether 'travel for consumption' will lead to activities that are more or less time-intensive. The individual may be as tempted by the larger houses available in a commuting town in Exurbia as he is by the possibility of sunning himself in a somewhat smaller back yard in Suburbia.

However, there is one analytical difference between education and commuting which may influence the effect of commuting on the labor-leisure choice. Most formal education is received at the beginning of the worker's life, then is repaid over his life span (in the form of higher earnings and improved consumer technology). An investment in commuting is made each day and is repaid each day by the daily wage. Since the investment is not large and fixed, the commuter is permitted a flexibility denied to the student. For example, the commuter may take all of his increased leisure in the form of fewer work days per week, longer vacations, and an earlier retirement, and none of it in shorter hours per day. Insofar as weekend leisure is a good substitute for a shorter work week, a commuting work force can have both high wages and more leisure. In that case commuting would affect the distribution of leisure time more than it would affect the aggregate level of leisure.

Problems of Measuring Commuting Time

The statistical data on hours of commuting time are much weaker than those on hours of work. Hours of work data permit leisure time plus travel time of employees to be measured with some confidence. The poor quality of the travel time data makes it more difficult to measure leisure net of commuting time.

In the empirical work of Chapter 5, approximate estimates of commuting time are employed. In any event, an analysis of cross-sectional data on hours traveled per worker in recent years shows that it is most unlikely that increases in travel time absorbed more than a fraction of the decline in hours worked at market employment.[44] While commuting makes the measurement of leisure time more difficult, it does not, at least, bias the income statistics (apart from travel fare), as does education, nor does it bias the price of leisure, as did fatigue and productive consumption.

Problems of Utilizing Commuting Time in a Model of the Demand for Leisure Time

One has little more success in estimating the changes in travel time from changes in known variables than one would have making such estimates of education. Higher real wage rates at all locations will lead to commuting at higher speeds and for longer distances, as they do to higher levels of education and a higher quality of education, but they need not lead to a greater amount of time spent in travel nor to a greater investment in time spent as a student.

A decline in the relative price of transportation at all speeds would again lead to greater speed and distance traveled, but not necessarily to more time in travel.[45]

44. See quantitative estimates made in John OWEN, 'The Supply of Labor' (unpublished Ph. D. dissertation, Columbia University, 1964).

45. In the second part of Mathematical Note 2-C an example is given in which changes of this sort in wage rates and in fares would have *no* effect on time spent in traveling. Even more to the point, in this example the optimizing elasticity of income with respect to hours of work plus travel time would be the same at all levels of hours of leisure and would not be affected by proportionate changes in the wage rate paid at all locations. However, if, perhaps as a result of the growth of cities, wages paid at long distances from one's home rose relative to those paid close to home, the elasticity of income with respect to effort-time would rise. But if the relative price of high-speed transportation to slower transportation also declined, then the optimizing elasticity of income with respect to work plus travel time would decline.

One type of price change that would affect the demand for commuting time would be one which would reduce the relative cost of *comfortable* travel. This should be analogous to an improvement in working conditions in its effects on the allocation of time, and would be expected to increase travel time.

The effect of government finance on the work-leisure choice has received almost as much attention from economists as has that of the wage rate, and it need only be outlined here.[46]

In its effects on those whose income is solely or mainly derived from their labor, a proportionate tax on income is analogous to a reduction in the wage rate. If there is a negative relation between hours of work and the wage rate, then the imposition of such a tax on wages should tend to increase hours of work. However, income taxes are rather progressive for the average wage earner in the United States, largely because of the system of exemptions. Thus, such taxes create diseconomies of scale in work and may tend to discourage effort.

It is not clear which effect will predominate. Those at the low end of the earnings scale pay no income taxes at all on the first thirty or forty hours of work per week, but their marginal rate is quite low (for these people the tax effect is similar to the fatigue effect, but much less important). Those further up the earnings scale have a higher marginal rate, but they begin to pay taxes after they have worked for only a few hours, and thus the income effect is much greater for them.

Perhaps the greatest disincentive to effort of such a system of taxation is that these taxes make top executive positions less attractive, relatively speaking, than lower paid jobs (except insofar as the market raises the pretax differentials to compensate for the tax). As a result, one would expect to find employees less eager to seek promotion through greater effort and longer hours of work.

One can probably abstract from the effects of other kinds of taxes on the average level of hours in an empirical analysis, if one first standardizes for changes in the real wage rate. Indirect taxes are in fact often passed on directly to the consumer in the form of higher prices

46. See, for example: George P. BREAK, 'Income Taxes, Wage Rates, and the Incentive to Supply Labor Services', *National Tax Journal*, VI (Dec., 1953), 333-52; Gershon COOPER, 'Taxation and Incentive in Mobilization', *Quarterly Journal of Economics*, LXVI (Feb., 1952), 43-66; W.J. CORBETT and D.C.HAGUE, 'Complementarity and the Excess Burden of Taxation', *Review of Economic Studies*, XXI (1953-1954), 21-30; A. C. HARBERGER, 'Taxation, Resource Allocation and Welfare', in *The Role of Direct and Indirect Taxes in the Federal Reserve System* (a Conference Report of the National Bureau of Economic Research and the Brookings Institution; Princeton: Princeton University Press, 1964); and F. W. PAISH, 'Economic Incentive in Wartime', *Economica*, VIII, NS (Aug., 1941), 239-48.

and rents. However, the conventional measure of real wages incorporates the effect of these taxes insofar as they raise the level of the Consumer Price Index. Similarly, some government expenditures are in the form of price-reducing subsidies, and no special analysis of their effects should be necessary here. An important exception arises when indirect taxes affect *relative* prices in such a way as to influence the labor-leisure choice. Thus, an excise tax on television sets or motion pictures may tend to reduce the demand for leisure time.

The effects of government expenditures are only a little less ambiguous than those of taxes. In general, goods and services provided by the government free would be analogous to non-labor income and might be expected to encourage leisure, if leisure is a superior good. However, these goods and services are not money, and their form may also affect the income-leisure choice. For example, the provision of a public school system by state and local government probably encourages work, rather than discouraging it.

2.11 HOURS OF WORK AND UNEMPLOYMENT

A full explanation of unemployment in an industrial, capitalist country must use macroeconomic a swell as microeconomic tools. However, given a certain deficit in aggregate demand (or demand for a particular sector of the labor market), a partial equilibrium analysis may be useful in understanding such questions as the distribution of the decline in aggregate demand between reductions in the number of employees and reductions in hours of work per employee.

It is in this context (i.e., where unemployment is regarded as an exogenous variable) that one can see a potentially important application of the principle of variable returns to the labor-leisure choice.

The notion that employees are first confronted with a market wage rate and then choose their hours of work, or that employers are indifferent to the level of hours worked in their businesses is not a useful abstraction in periods of widespread unemployment. Such periods are characterized by a shortage of work which extends to hours per worker, as well as to the total number of jobs. Labor markets are often quite disorganized at such times, and there is a considerable variance in employer reaction to the changed conditions.

A few employers may, in the interest of minimizing short-run losses, take full advantage of their bargaining power, lowering wages and raising hours of work until their workers' real income and leisure time are reduced to a subsistence level. Another group of employers may behave in a paternalistic fashion, absorbing much of the loss themselves, maintaining the wage level, and doling out employment and extra hours of work to those employees whose need is greatest.

However, one need not assume non-profit-maximizing behavior in order to explain the pro-cyclical fluctuations in hours of work per worker that characterize the demand for labor of the typical firm. Most employers have an investment in their employees in the form of on-the-job training and other personnel costs. The probability of losing this investment goes up more rapidly if the employee is laid off than if his hours of work are reduced (within limits). Hence, the rational employer may incline towards hours reduction.

Why, then, are employees ever laid off? If employers lower hours far enough, they begin to lose employees through resignations. Moreover, the morale of those who remain deteriorates. The rational employer may reason that the same morale, or quit, effect would be produced by a wage reduction with no cut in hours. He therefore must balance the cost of training new employees against the cost (in wages) of keeping the old ones.

Equal total labor cost (TLC) curves for an employer in such a position are shown in Figures 2-H-1 and 2-H-2. In Figure 2-H-1, costs per

FIGURE 2-H
Unemployment and hours of work

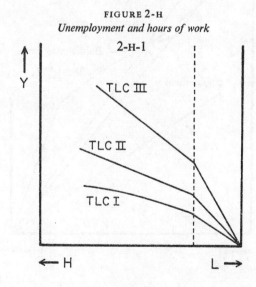

53

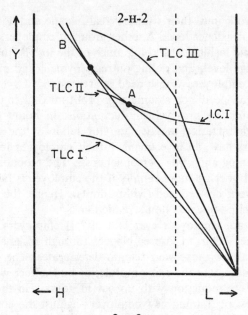

2-H-2

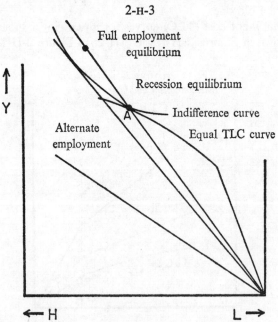

2-H-3

Full employment
equilibrium

Recession equilibrium

Indifference curve

Alternate
employment

Equal TLC curve

layoff are constant; in the second, they are a rising function of the number of layoffs. Let B in Figure 2-H-2 be the alternative employment possibility for the average employee. Then the employer may choose any combination of hours and income equivalent to employment B (in satisfaction to the employee).[47] These are represented on indifference curve (IC)1. In this diagram, the employer minimizes his total labor costs by choosing point A.[48]

When one examines the hours and wages data of depressed periods, one finds that while there is a striking reduction in hours of work, price declines offset wage cuts so that, on the average, there is little evidence of a reduction in the real hourly wage. Equilibrium for a typical firm under such circumstances is shown in Figure 2-H-3. Note that if the firm is to offer hours longer than A, in order to keep unit labor costs constant it must still pay an hourly wage that is less than that paid for a shorter hours schedule.

In the real world, this model would have to be modified in a number of important respects. The employer's expectation of an eventual end to the recession or depression will not only affect his evaluation of re-hiring costs but will also bring into consideration the improved bargaining position that his employees will have in a tighter labor market. Thus, he must consider the future value of present good will. This will probably further incline him towards hours cutback as a method of apportioning his shrunken labor requirements.

Again, in a depressed labor market, the employee can often obtain a much higher 'alternative' wage if he is willing to search for it. The correct specification of the alternative wage would then be that wage finally chosen, net of search costs.[49] Moreover, the employee has a third option, that of accepting the hours reduction at the original job and seeking a second or part-time job. This extra work will require some search and will probably pay less than the original job but may still be an acceptable solution for many workers.[50]

47. This assumes that the employer is in a position to lay down terms to the employee, an assumption which is probably realistic enough in times of recession.
48. If he were not concerned about rehiring costs, he might choose point B, thus minimizing his payroll costs.
49. See G. STIGLER, 'The Economics of Information', and 'Information in the Labor Market', *Journal of Political Economy*, LXX (Supplement, October, 1962), 94-105.
50. See OWEN, 'The Supply of Labor', pp. 72-77.

If one introduces the notion of employee expectations, one finds more reasons for thinking that the employee will accept an hours reduction. If the worker rejects the reduction and quits his job to find a more normal schedule elsewhere at a lower hourly wage, he will then be confronted, at the end of the recession, with the necessity of changing jobs once again. Since job-hopping is costly to the worker as well as to the employer, he will be deterred from making the move if he thinks that the recession will be short-lived.

While these factors make it clear that the analysis of hours determination in times of unemployment is more complicated than was shown in the original statement,[51] they confirm rather than contradict the notion that, in times of recession, the value to the employer of an additional hour of an employee's time is less than that of a regularly scheduled hour, and that while a cutback in hours does have an income effect on the worker, the reduction in the tradeoff of income for leisure on the margin is the dominant factor in the average employee's decision to accept shorter hours of work.

Unemployment and Hours of Work of the Self-Employed

Hours of work of the self-employed, or at least those in family-sized farms or businesses, will not be subjected to the same influences as those of employees. If the ratio of the value of the marginal hour to the average hour worked does decline, the decline may be caused by a change in the elasticity of demand for the firm's product at a given level of output.

But if a competitive model is used (as would be appropriate for a large proportion of the self-employed), it is hard to see why there should be any tendency for hours of family-sized enterprises to be reduced during a recession.[52] In fact, the reduction of profits (or the proliferation of losses) incident upon a recession may have a powerful

51. Some of these factors are discussed further in *ibid.*, pp. 83-85, along with an analysis of changes since 1929 in the determinants of hours in periods of unemployment.
52. One exception would arise if the family found that prices and costs had changed in such a way that it could not cover non-labor costs on certain types of business activities but that it could afford certain others. Unless the type of activity dropped could be easily replaced by another, this would mean a cutback in the size of the business. Other exceptions would of course arise, as monopolies and other non-competitive market structures are considered.

56

income effect, forcing the family to work long hours to avoid bankruptcy.

Thus, in a recession one would expect a divergence between hours worked by employees and by the self-employed.

2.12 THE ANALYSIS OF THE DEMAND FOR LEISURE TIME: SOME IMPLICATIONS FOR EMPIRICAL RESEARCH

Leisure and Work Activities: The Price of Recreation

Leisure time and market recreation appear to be closely related in consumption. The outputs of the commercial recreation industry are used during leisure time. A substantial proportion of leisure time is devoted to recreation.

One might then expect an empirically observable relationship to exist between developments in the recreation industry and the demand for leisure time. Moreover, consumer demand theory provides us with straightforward empirical tests of this relationship: the demand for leisure time can be estimated as a function of the price of recreation, and the demand for recreation estimated as a function of the price of leisure. Negative relationships between the demand for leisure time (recreation) and the price of recreation (leisure time) would be evidence of complementarity between the two goods. Positive relationships would support the hypothesis that they were substitutes.

The analysis of leisure as an activity broadens the discussion to regard leisure time and commercial recreation as inputs into consumer activities. An immediate result of this way of looking at leisure is that it presents the possibility that leisure and recreation may be used together, and, in fact, be closely related in almost every sense of that term, yet a change in the price of one might have no effect on the demand for the other. For example, no relationship would exist between the price of recreation and the demand for leisure time if a decline in the recreation price induced an expansion of the demand for leisure activity that was just offset by a substitution in the input mix against leisure time. This suggests that it is worthwhile to examine the elasticity of substitution directly. This might be done in a model in which one can observe the effect of a change in the price of leisure relative to the price of recreation on the proportion in which leisure and recreation are consumed.

57

Leisure and Work Activities: Working Conditions

The quality of working conditions is also related to the demand for leisure time. Changes in the employer cost (net of productivity benefits) of providing good working conditions might be positively related to the demand for leisure time, and negatively related to the quality of working conditions. However, this employer cost variable differs from the market price of recreation variable in that working conditions are not bought and sold on a market in the same fashion as are the products of the commercial recreation industry (or other consumer goods). As the analysis in section 2.2 made clear, it would be most difficult to obtain empirical measures of the employer net cost of providing good working conditions.

The Price of Leisure Time

The analysis in this chapter has shown that the price of leisure time is not simply equal to the wage rate; it is a negative function of unemployment and fatigue, and, at low levels of income, a positive function of productive consumption. Government taxation and spending programs also affect the price of leisure (as well as income), although it is difficult to determine the net effect of government activity on the demand for leisure time.

In order to measure the price of leisure time more accurately, wage rate data must at least be supplemented by estimates of the effects of both fatigue and unemployment.

Moreover, the hourly wage rate itself is a positive function of education and commuting time. The analysis in this chapter suggests that the income-leisure choice is biased by the development of attractive commuting and educational possibilities, most probably in the direction of income. The measurement of income and leisure (though not of the price of leisure) is distorted by the existence of a high level of commuting and education among the work force.

The Use of This Analysis in the Following Chapters

The analysis of the demand for leisure time in this chapter provides the basis for the empirical models tested in Chapter 5.

The apparently close connection in consumption between leisure time and recreation suggested that this relationship should be an im-

58

portant focus of the empirical work. Data on prices and quantities for the recreation industry were collected and used in the statistical work in Chapter 5. The relationship was explored in a leisure activity model, as well as by estimating the demand for leisure time as a function of the price of recreation, and then the demand for recreation as a function of the price of leisure time. The elasticity of substitution between leisure and recreation was measured by estimating the proportions in which they are consumed as a function of their relative prices.

In the empirical estimation of the price of leisure here, fatigue was incorporated by comparing models that assume that output increases with hours of work at a decreasing rate with a model in which hours and output increase proportionately.[53] The effects of unemployment were measured in several ways, including the use of an iterative model in which an attempt was made to select the correct relationship between unemployment and the price of leisure on the basis of correlation results.

Because of the great difficulties in collecting data on the employer net cost of providing good working conditions and the proliferation of good educational and commuting opportunities, these variables were omitted from the empirical analysis.

However, an estimate of commuting time was added to work time so as to reduce the bias in the measurement of leisure time. Similarly, the use of annual leisure, rather than lifetime leisure estimates minimizes the measurement bias induced by the omission of education time.

In order to proceed with the empirical analysis, data were collected from unpublished as well as published sources. Chapter 3 describes the data collection process for the leisure time estimates and also gives a description of the major short-run movements in the series.

Similarly, Chapter 4 describes the movements in prices and production of the major commercial recreation industries, as well as giving the methods used in data collection.

Wage and unemployment rate data were more readily available, and are described briefly in section 5.1.a.

The reader who is more interested in the regression and correlation

---

53. The omission of models in which output rises more than proportionately to hours implies the assumption that incomes were high enough in the twentieth century, in the United States, for the fatigue effect to dominate the productive consumption effect.

analysis of the demand for leisure time and the demand for recreation, rather than in the movements of the several variables, may skip these sections, and move directly to the discussion of empirical models in Chapter 5.

CHAPTER 3

THE DEMAND FOR LEISURE TIME: THE DATA

3.1 INTRODUCTION

Time series estimates are developed in this chapter of the leisure time of employees in the United States, 1900-1961. These data (along with the recreation data in Chapter 4) are used in regression and correlation analyses in Chapter 5 to examine several of the hypotheses about the demand for leisure time which were presented in Chapter 2. The reader who is primarily interested in the results of this work might then omit Chapters 3 and 4, and move directly to the discussion of empirical models in Chapter 5.

Leisure time per employee is measured here on an annual basis. Section 3.2 describes the major long and short run movements in hours of work per week since 1900. Section 3.3 describes the spread of vacations and holidays. These data are then combined to form estimates of annual work time. Finally, leisure time estimates are presented in section 5.1.b. Because most of the increase in demand for leisure time in the United States since 1900 has come about from changes in annual leisure time, this time series was then used as an estimate of total leisure demand.[1]

3.2 HOURS WORKED PER WEEK, 1900-1961

The annual estimates of weekly hours given in Table 3-A show that while the 1890's had been a period of relative stagnation in the drive for shorter hours,[2] the first fifteen years of the twentieth century saw a

1. See pp. 8-12 above.
2. H. A. MILLIS and R. E. MONTGOMERY, *The Economics of Labor* (N.Y.: McGraw-Hill Book Co., 1938-1945), III, 469.

revival in the movement. Unionized industries led the way, comparing favorably both in respect to level and to size of reduction in hours. However, the much larger non-unionized sector also obtained important reductions.[3] In the second decade of this century the movement towards shorter hours accelerated.

The eight hour agitation became increasingly vigorous between 1890 and 1914 ... Beginning in 1914 and 1915 ... the eight hour movement seemed literally to sweep the country. The crystallization of public sentiment was manifested when President Wilson declared that the American people had made up their minds in favor of the eight hour day.[4]

Hours reductions in this pre-World War I period are usually depicted by historians as moderate, especially when the non-union sector is being described. Actually, the total decline of 6 percent that is observed in hours in the 1900-1913 period (see Table 3-A) is rather large when one considers that real wages in this period rose somewhat slowly.

A constitutional, general hours act was not possible in the United States before the Supreme Court approval of the Fair Labor Standards Act of 1938.[5] However, when the United States entered World War I, and government contracts mushroomed throughout industry, the Eight Hours Act of 1912 (as amended by the Naval Appropriations Act of 1917), providing for the eight-hour day (i.e., for the forty-eight hour week) with time and a half paid for overtime on government contract work, had a very wide effect on the economy.

It is impossible to separate the influence of this Eight Hours Act on hours reduction in World War I from that of the abnormally high demand for labor brought about by the war itself. As Leo Wolman said: 'Reductions in hours during the World War and in similar periods of intense business activity were in part the result of competition among industries for labor; for in such periods, concessions in hours, like

3. See P.H.DOUGLAS, *Real Wages in the U.S., 1890-1926* (Boston: Pollak Foundation for Economic Research, 1930), pp. 113, 115.
4. MILLIS and MONTGOMERY, *The Economics of Labor*, p. 469.
5. Marion CAHILL'S *Shorter Hours* (N.Y.: Columbia University Press, 1932), esp. Chapter III, 'National Legislation'. Throughout the book Cahill refers to the movement for a national hours act as utopian.

increases in wage rates, reflected the state of the labor market.' [6]

The excellent market for labor benefited those sectors of the economy controlled by trade unions. During the war, reductions in hours and other benefits were gained without strikes. To obtain these same benefits 'in other periods strikes have been protracted and have reached staggering costs.' [7]

Moreover, in the view of Marion Cahill:

Labor's appreciation of the basic [8] eight hour day as a means of drawing some of the war profits from manufacturers did not obscure for them the larger view that it was establishing the principle of a straight eight hour day for the time when peace should have removed the need for excessive production. With both the immediate and the ultimate advantage of the basic eight hour day in view labor used its strategic position to spread its adoption. In this it was aided by the War Labor Board, which almost invariably awarded the basic eight hour day when the question of hours was at issue.[9]

From 1913 to 1919 weekly hours fell by 4.5 hours or about 8 percent. In the following decade, they fell by less than two hours. The nineteen twenties was a period of moderately low unemployment and of rapidly rising wages (see Table 5-A). Yet full-time or standard hours in manufacturing and other industries showed little net change.[10] It would seem that this stagnation was at least in part a reaction to the hot-house growth of the movement toward shorter hours during World War I.

Wolman's analysis of full-time hours in manufacturing shows that

The proportion employed on the 48 hour week appeared to decline from 1919 to 1929, while the percentage of those working from 49 to 54 hours,

6. Leo WOLMAN, *Hours of Work in American Industry*, Bulletin Number 71 of the National Bureau of Economic Research (N.Y.: National Bureau of Economic Research, 1938), p. 2.

7. CAHILL, *Shorter Hours*, p. 26.

8. The 'basic eight hour day' meant that time and a half must be paid for work over eight hours. The 'straight eight hour day' meant that no work over eight hours was allowed.

9. CAHILL, *Shorter Hours*, p. 81.

10. See WOLMAN, *Hours of Work in American Industry*, for manufacturing, and John KENDRICK, *Productivity Trends in the United States*, National Bureau of Economic Research, General Series, Number 71 (Princeton: Princeton University Press, 1961), for discussions of full-time hours in the nineteen twenties in different industries.

presumably on a 50 hour week, increased quite considerably. It may be said that a substantial number of the employees who had their hours reduced to 48 or fewer during the War surrendered a considerable part of their gains during the decade 1919-1929.[11]

However, the statistical evidence shows that the nineteen twenties was also a period of standardization of hours. The iron and steel industry finally abandoned the twelve-hour day in 1923. Other industries, such as canning and preserving, sugar refining, and lumber, which had retained unusually long full-time hours during the war, reduced them materially from 1922 to 1929.[12] The net statistical result of these increases and decreases was a virtual arrest in the progress towards a shorter work week.

In the general collapse of traditional hours schedules in the nineteen thirties (see Table 3-A) a superimposed drop in 1934 is observable, followed by a rise in 1935 and 1936. This occurred despite the fact that unemployment reached its peak in 1933 and that movements in hours usually lead, not follow, unemployment.[13] This drop was probably due to the operation of the National Recovery Administration hours codes, which provided for maximum working hours of forty or less per week in most industries covered.[14]

The data in the text table below are as presented by Millis and Montgomery: [15]

| | Average hours worked per week | |
	Manufacturing	All industries
January, 1932	38.4	42.1
January, 1933	37.5	41.5
June, 1933	42.6	43.9

11. WOLMAN, *Hours of Work in American Industry*, p. 7.

12. *Ibid.*, p. 20. See also OWEN, 'Reduction in Hours'. Important experiments in the five-day week did take place in the nineteen twenties. Most of the innovators who reduced hours, with the exception of Henry Ford, did so under pressure from closed shop unions. See National Industrial Conference Board Studies, Number 148, *The Five Day Week in Manufacturing* (N.Y.: National Industrial Conference Board, 1929)

13. Gerhard BRY, *The Average Workweek as an Economic Indicator*, Occasional Paper Number 69 of the National Bureau of Economic Research (N.Y.: National Bureau of Economic Research, 1959).

14. MILLIS and MONTGOMERY, *The Economics of Labor*, pp. 481-83.

15. *Ibid.*, p. 481 and p. 485.

January, 1934	33.7	37.5
June, 1934	34.9	37.4
January, 1935	35.2	37.6
November, 1935	37.8	39.3
June, 1936	39.2	39.2
November, 1936	40.6	40.6

The 1933 increase during the period January to June probably reflected the normal upward influence of the cycle, and perhaps seasonal factors as well. Millis and Montgomery attribute the rise in hours to the 'consequence of the tendency during the first half of 1933 to abandon the share-the-work movement and let any increase in labor hours effectuate itself through a lengthening of the average time of those employed rather than through hiring more workers . . .'.[16]

The hours codes went into effect in 1933. They were invalidated in the Schechter decision in 1935. The data do seem to support the conclusion that the N.R.A. had an important, if short-lived,[17] effect on hours.

The extension of hours after the invalidation of N.R.A. was cut short by two developments that have radically altered the institutions of hours determination in the United States.

The first was the quantitative extension of unionism following the passage of the Wagner Act and the formation of the Committee for Industrial Organization in 1935. Trade union membership as a percentage of non-agricultural employment rose from 13 percent in 1935 to 28 percent in 1938.

The second was the passage of the Fair Labor Standards Act in 1938 (and, what is much more important, the subsequent Supreme Court decision that declared it constitutional), which provided for time and one-half payment in covered employment for work over forty-four hours a week in 1938, forty-two hours in 1939, and forty hours as of October, 1940.[18]

One can probably see the immediate effect of these changes in the

16. *Ibid.*, p. 484.
17. But see MILLIS and MONTGOMERY: 'There can be no question that many more employers are resigned today (1938) to the thought of a 40 or 44 hour week and of a 5 day week than were so resigned in 1928 or 1929' (*ibid.*, p. 485).
18. C. W. WRIGHT, *Economic History of the U.S.* (N.Y.: McGraw-Hill Book Co., 1940).

fact that average weekly hours declined by almost one hour from 1936 to 1940 despite a reduction in unemployment from 17.0 percent to 14.6 percent.

In many industrial plants, however, these depression-induced measures either confirmed or at most exaggerated the low schedule of hours arising out of the disequilibrium situation of the nineteen thirties. The real influence of the forty-hour law and of extensive unionization was to be seen in the full employment conditions prevailing during and especially after World War II.

The F.L.S.A. hours law in World War II seemed to function in much the same manner as did the 1912 act in World War I, that is, 'as a means of drawing some of the war profits' into the hands of the wage-earning class. However, hours per worker rose during World War II, indicating that employer demand was strong enough to permit the payment of time and one-half premiums. This situation is in contrast to that prevailing in World War I, when, according to these data, average hours actually fell.

Thus World War II ended with hours at a rather high level rather than at an abnormally low one. Moreover, the F.L.S.A., unlike the 1912 eight-hour law, covered non-government as well as government work, and hence its application was not curtailed by the cessation of hostilities.

A third factor distinguishing the recent postwar period from the nineteen twenties was the retention by the unions, at least temporarily, of their wartime membership [19] and their important role in hours determination.

However, the forty-hour level, appropriate as it might have been to 1938 conditions of employment and income, was perhaps 'ahead of its time' in the event of full employment and 1938 (or even 1946) income levels.

Given these conditions, it was predictable [20] that, with the ending of the wartime labor market in 1945, hours should drop rapidly towards the forty-hour level, and that this drop should be followed by a period of relative stagnation in the movement towards shorter hours.

19. U.S., Bureau of the Census, *Historical Statistics of the U.S.: Colonial Times to 1957*, p. 98, gives union membership as a percentage of non-agricultural employment: in 1935, 13.4 percent; in 1938, 27.8 percent; in 1940, 27.2 percent; in 1945, 35.8 percent; in 1950, 31.9 percent; and in 1955, 33.6 percent.
20. Assuming, of course, that one could predict there would not be a depression or a war, that hourly wages would continue to rise, etc.

Hours dropped from 48.2 in 1944 to 43.7 in 1946, and then declined more slowly to 42.3 in 1961.[21]

TABLE 3-A

Average hours worked per week by private, non-agricultural wage and salary workers in the United States, 1900-1961 *

Year	Hours	Year	Hours	Year	Hours
1900	58.5	1921	48.4	1942	44.3
1901	58.4	1922	48.9	1943	46.8
1902	58.1	1923	49.6	1944	46.9
1903	57.9	1924	48.8	1945	45.6
1904	57.1	1925	49.0	1946	43.3
1905	57.2	1926	49.3	1947	42.4
1906	57.0	1927	49.1	1948	41.7
1907	56.9	1928	48.8	1949	41.0
1908	55.6	1929	48.7	1950	41.1
1909	55.7	1930	47.1	1951	41.7
1910	55.6	1931	45.6	1952	42.0
1911	55.4	1932	43.7	1953	41.5
1912	55.3	1933	43.3	1954	40.4
1913	55.0	1934	40.6	1955	41.6
1914	54.0	1935	41.7	1956	41.9
1915	53.4	1936	43.4	1957	41.2
1916	53.8	1937	43.1	1958	40.9
1917	53.4	1938	41.6	1959	40.8
1918	52.4	1939	42.1	1960	41.0
1919	50.0	1940	42.5	1961	41.2
1920	50.6	1941	43.3		

* Hours of work of non-student males adjusted for vacations and holidays, 1940-1961; students and women included in the data 1900-1940. No adjustment made in the earlier period for vacations and holidays. The two series are linked at 1940 by raising the earlier series.
Source: See text.

21. Based on figures for non-student males, not adjusted for vacations and holidays. See column 2 of Table 3-B.

TABLE 3-B

*Adjustment of hours data for vacations and holidays
and for changes in labor force composition*

Year	All workers Total hours (1)	Non-student male workers	
		Total hours (2)	Adjusted hours (3)
1940	41.9	43.1	42.5
1941	42.8	44.0	43.3
1942	43.6	45.1	44.3
1943	45.4	47.3	46.8
1944	45.9	48.2	46.9
1945	44.1	46.4	45.6
1946	41.6	43.7	43.3
1947	41.2	43.2	42.4
1948	40.9	43.1	41.7
1949	40.7	42.9	41.0
1950	40.3	42.8	41.1
1951	40.9	43.4	41.7
1952	40.5	43.0	42.0
1953	40.2	42.7	41.5
1954	39.6	42.3	40.4
1955	39.9	42.8	41.6
1956	39.7	42.9	41.9
1957	39.5	42.6	41.2
1958	38.9	42.2	40.8
1959	39.3	42.5	40.8
1960	39.1	42.5	41.0
1961	38.7	42.3	41.2

Source: See pp. 73-75 for derivation of hours data for non-student males (total hours and hours adjusted for vacations and holidays).

3.3 GAINS IN VACATIONS AND HOLIDAYS SINCE 1940

The 1929 to 1961 period was marked by an increase in the number of workers taking paid annual vacations from a minority to a large majority of all workers in the United States. The number of holidays taken per year also rose sharply during this period.

Vacations and holidays are, of course, a form of leisure and should be added to the leisure arising from reductions in the work week. To accomplish this, annual estimates of vacation and holiday time since 1940 were converted into weekly equivalents and subtracted from the work week to obtain a quantitative estimate of the increase in aggregate leisure.

Paid vacations and holidays were not common among blue-collar workers in the United States in the prewar period, though they were more usual among office employees.

Vacations were traditionally the special prerogative of those who worked in the office. Their work went on whether the shop worked full time or not, and they had no free time unless it was specially provided. Shop work being more irregular, its workers often had time off (without pay) although their freedom to use it was cramped by the requirement that they be available for work on short notice. Important holidays were not worked – or paid – the economic effect being the same as a disciplinary layoff.[22]

This pattern began to change in the late nineteen thirties, with an employer here and there yielding to union demands for paid vacations. The rate of change was greatly accelerated during World War II.[23]

The Bureau of Labor Statistics found, in a study of collective bargaining contracts in 1940,[24] that 'an estimated 2,000,000 union members, or approximately 25 percent of all organized wage earners in the United States receive annual vacations with pay under collective agreements with their employers.' The report implied that the unionized sector fared somewhat better than the unorganized sector with regard to vacations. Allen maintains [25] that the reverse was true, that in fact 50 percent of all wage earners then had vacations.

Vacations and holidays spread rapidly under the special conditions of World War II.

The adoption of vacation provisions was stimulated during World War II by

---

22. A. KUHN, *Labor: Economics and Institutions* (N.Y.: Rinehart, 1956), pp. 223-24. See also D. ALLEN, *Fringe Benefits: Wages or Social Obligation?* (Ithaca: Cornell University Press, 1964).
23. *Ibid.*
24. 'Vacations with Pay in Union Agreements, 1940', U.S., Bureau of Labor Statistics, *Monthly Labor Review*, LXII (1940), 1070-77.
25. D. ALLEN, *Fringe Benefits*, p. 85.

the National War Labor Board's wage stabilization policy. This policy was more lenient with regard to wage supplements than with wage increases. The standard Board policy was one week's vacation for one year of service and two weeks for five years or more ... Before World War II, paid holidays for wage earners in the manufacturing, construction and mining industries were found in a few collective bargaining agreements. The practice of granting paid holidays to production workers has grown rapidly since. Again, the N.W.L.B. of World War II is credited with giving impetus to the trend. Its policy permitted approval of voluntary applications for pay for as many as six holidays not worked. Since wage rate adjustments were tightly controlled, many unions and employers negotiated holiday pay clauses.[26]

In the years immediately after the war, 1946 and 1947, vacation agreements were extended to several important mass production industries, and by 1949 the principle of paid vacation for wage earners was firmly established.[27] By 1957, 92 percent of union contracts covering one thousand or more employees contained provisions for paid vacations,[28] and by 1961, the Bureau of Labor Statistics was able to state that 'practically all office and plant workers in the country's metropolitan areas are now entitled to paid vacations.'[29]

Moreover, the length of vacation has been increased. While the typical blue-collar vacation provision in 1940 was a flat one-week vacation after one year's service,[30] it is now typical to offer a graduated scale depending on length of service. The Bureau of Labor Statistics Metropolitan Area Survey (taken June 30, 1961)[31] showed that plant workers for the most part received one week's vacation after one year's service, two weeks after five years' service, and three weeks after fifteen years' service. Provisions for office workers are somewhat more generous.

At the same time there was an important growth in the number of holidays taken. The Bureau of Labor Statistics estimates that, for the

26. A. L. GITLOW, *Labor Economics and Industrial Relations* (Homewood, Ill.: Richard D. Irwin, 1957).
27. 'Paid Vacations in Major Union Contracts in 1957', U.S., Bureau of Labor Statistics, *Monthly Labor Review*, LXXX (1958), 744.
28. *Ibid.*
29. Peter HENLE, 'Recent Growth of Paid Leisure for U.S. Workers', U.S., Bureau of Labor Statistics, *Monthly Labor Review*, LXXXIV (1962), 249-57.
30. *Monthly Labor Review*, LI (1940).
31. *Monthly Labor Review*, LXXXV (1962), p. 255.

labor force as a whole, the number of paid holidays rose from two per year in 1940 to six per year in 1960.[32]

Table 3-B shows hours data, adjusted for vacations and holidays. The adjusted data give a better picture of the annual leisure time of employees than do unadjusted weekly hours data.

3.4 LONGER VACATIONS OR SHORTER HOURS? AN ANALYSIS

One way to analyze the shift from shorter weekly hours to vacations and holidays as a method of increasing leisure is to regard both of these as parts of a broader continuum of changes in leisure time. Increases in the proportion of time spent by an individual in leisure or consumption may be brought about by cuts in hours worked per day, days per week, weeks per year, or years out of one's life. It is fairly obvious that American workers have taken, and continue to take, their increases in leisure in each of these ways. We see movement toward a seven-hour day, a four-day week, a one-month vacation, and retirement at age sixty.

Much of the increase in leisure time since World War I, or at least since the nineteen twenties,[33] has been in the form of fewer days worked per week, or fewer weeks per year, rather than in fewer hours per day. Thus, along with a trend toward more leisure time, the empirical evidence points to a tendency toward taking that leisure in larger chunks.

It is unlikely that this sequencing of leisure time gains represents a random pattern. While there is no pretense here of a complete explanation of this shift, the following economic factors would be expected to be important.

It was argued on pages 30-35 that the reduction of hours of work to about eight per day has an immediate, positive effect on productivity per hour (as well as possible long-run effects). But some experts, at least, feel that further reductions in the work day would at best have smaller positive productivity effects.[34]

The introduction of paid vacations and holidays also has positive effects on productivity. These effects were, in fact, an important or

32. *Ibid.*
33. By the end of this decade the eight or eight and one-half hour day had become standard for a large proportion of workers.
34. See NORTHRUP and BRINBERG, *Economics of the Workweek.*

even decisive factor in the early introduction of vacations by pioneering managements. However, the quantitative gain in hourly output as a result of an annual vacation is relatively difficult to measure. Moreover, if there is a high turnover in the work force, a large proportion of the company's investment in worker refreshment is lost to other employers.[35]

Thus, if employers were to choose how to reduce hours of work per year per employee at the least cost in output, one would expect them first to reduce hours of work per day to eight or so, and only then to explore the use of paid vacations and holidays as a method of increasing employee leisure.

Moreover, apart from these productivity arguments, there are certain economies of scale in work time and in leisure time that might induce employees to choose a mix of hours reduction techniques, rather than a straightforward cut in daily hours.

Admittedly, the first concern of an employee is to obtain enough time each day to sleep, eat, and rest for the next day's work. But once these basic needs are satisfied, it becomes possible to take advantage of economies of scale in the utilization of leisure time. A whole day off permits the employee to engage in many leisure or consumption activities that would not otherwise be feasible. Moreover, it provides a certain psychic removal from the work situation. These factors were considered in providing Sunday rest,[36] Sunday plus Saturday afternoon rest, and now Saturday and Sunday [37] off each week and six holidays per year.

These economies of scale in leisure time are even more obvious when one considers larger sets of days off, i.e., vacations. Ordinarily, physical and psychological removal from everyday surroundings is only possible in annual vacations: transportation costs would make it impossible, or at least not economical, over a two-day weekend.[38]

Economies of scale in work also become important to the worker when there are fixed costs of a day's work. These would include ex-

35. These problems are discussed in ALLEN, *Fringe Benefits*, p. 80. Apparently they influenced management to give vacations first to those employees who were known to be refreshed by vacations (i.e., management) and last to those groups which had a high turnover rate.

36. Or Sabbath holiday. These customs are, of course, an important part of our Judaeo-Christian tradition.

37. National Industrial Conference Board, *The Five Day Week in Manufacturing*.

38. These more ambitious ways of using leisure time also require more money. Hence,

72

penditures in time and money in getting to and from work, and the additional expense of eating a lunch away from home. This factor would also discourage reduction in daily hours beyond a certain point.[39]

3.5 CORRECTION OF DISTORTIONS INTRODUCED INTO THE LEISURE TIME MEASURE BY INCREASED EMPLOYMENT OF WOMEN AND STUDENTS

If the main work activity of employees is their market work, then a time series of hours worked per week by persons employed in the market sector might be a good substitute for their total hours of work per week, and might even be a fair substitute for hours of work of students, housewives, or others employed in non-market sectors. This view gains some support from a comparison of time budgets (see Table 4-A, p. 82, below) which shows leisure patterns for male workers, housewives, and students.

However, market work data become a poor measure of total leisure or work when there emerges a third class – those who are employed in both market and non-market activities. This third group may have exactly the same leisure pattern as the first two, but its emergence will produce a downward bias in the hours statistics.

In fact, if this third group does have the same leisure-work distribution, the percentage of relative distortion in the hours measure will be equal to the proportion of the labor force engaged in both market and non-market activities, multiplied by the proportion of its work time that this group devotes to non-market activities.

This may be shown as follows:

Group	Number of workers engaged		Hours of work per worker		
	Market	Non-market	Market	Non-market	Total
I: Market	M	0	X	0	X
II: Non-Market	0	N	0	X	X
III: Combined	C	C	$(1-a)X$	aX	X

The measured hours average, $Y = \dfrac{MX + C(1-a)X}{M+C}$

one reason why paid vacations for workers came late in American economic development may be that vacation time is more valuable to workers when they have the funds to remove themselves from their everyday surroundings.

39. National Industrial Conference Board, *The Five Day Week in Manufacturing*, p. 26.

Letting R equal the proportion of Group III in the labor force ($R = \dfrac{C}{M+C}$), the downward relative bias of the measured work week ($\dfrac{X-Y}{X}$) will be equal to aR, the share of hours worked devoted to non-market work by Group III times the proportion of Group III in the labor force (Group I + Group III). Both a and R have been rising in the past twenty-two years, creating a downward bias in the hours series.

In this period at least two groups in the labor force with 'dual allegiance' (i.e., with heavy non-labor force commitments) have become important: married women and students. Moreover, the evidence shows that the newer labor force recruits from these groups tend to have fewer hours to spare for market work than had the earlier recruits.

The share of women in non-agricultural wage and salary employment rose from 30 percent in 1940 to 32 percent in 1950 to 36 percent in 1960.[40] By that date, the male non-agricultural worker averaged about seven hours of work a week more than the female.[41] The development of a sector of the labor force working fewer than average hours in the market sector will of course result in a downward movement in the measured average.

Moreover, the male-female hours differential has risen from less than three hours in 1940 to over seven hours in 1962.[42] The increase in this differential has further contributed to the decline in measured average hours.

Much of this increase in the male-female hours differential is undoubtedly due to changes that took place in the composition of the female labor force. Thus, the percentage of 'married women, husband present' in the female labor force rose from 30 percent in 1940 to 55 percent in 1960. Moreover, within this category the proportion of wives with small children has risen, so that by 1961 over one-fifth of the working wives (husband present) had children under six years old, and over one-half of them had children under eighteen years. An increasing percentage of female employees, therefore, have substantial non-market liens on their time.

---

40. Statistics on employed women and students and, in particular, statistics on employed housewives and young students are quite weak for the early part of this period. The measurement of the employment of the marginal worker (in this context he who works only a few hours a week) was improved in the nineteen forties.
41. OWEN, 'The Supply of Labor', p. 173.
42. *Ibid.*, p. 174.

Because of the difficult problems raised by the varying household responsibilities of the different classes of female employees, women were eliminated altogether from the hours calculations.

Employed students are another group for whom the statistics of hours worked per week at their (usually part-time) jobs give a grossly misleading picture of their actual work-time choice. This group has grown in importance since 1940. Students constituted about 1 percent of wage and salary workers in non-agricultural industries in 1940. This percentage rose sharply during the tight labor markets of World War II and the Korean War, reaching a peak of 3.3 percent in 1950; it then receded to 2.3 percent in 1953. Since then the share of students in male non-agricultural wage and salary employment has risen to over 4 percent.

These increases have been due, on the one hand, to a rise in the labor force participation of students and, on the other hand, to expanding school enrollment. In 1940 to 1950, measured civilian labor force participation rates of students rose dramatically, but in the following decade there was no net change. The dramatic rise in student employment in the nineteen fifties is thus due entirely to increased school enrollment of teenage and college-age youth.[43]

There is, moreover, evidence that the average measured hours worked by employed students has declined. This downward movement is partially explained by the younger average age of student workers and by the better methods used by interviewers to obtain data on students who work a few hours a week.

The increased employment of students would seem to represent, if anything, a diminution rather than an increase in leisure. But rising student employment reduces the measured work week, thus distorting the measure. Since students, by definition, have non-market obligations, and since their study time is not really leisure or consumption time, the student group was also eliminated from the hours calculations.

Table 3-B, column 2, shows average hours worked per week by non-student males in non-agricultural wage and salary employment. Column 3 shows the figures adjusted for vacations and holidays. A comparison of the non-student male figures with those in column 1 shows that the conventional measure overestimates the reduction in work time that took place.

43. For student labor force participation rates, see U.S., Bureau of Labor Statistics, *Monthly Labor Review*, LXXXIII (1961), 708; U.S., Department of Commerce, *Current Population Reports*, Series P-50, Number 83.

3.6 CONCLUSIONS

1. Hours of work per employee have declined in the United States throughout the twentieth century. Hours of work have moved pro-cyclically, reaching very low levels in the nineteen thirties.

2. While most of the earlier reductions in hours worked were in weekly hours, more recent gains have been concentrated in vacations and holidays. This may be explained, in part at least, by the operation of the fatigue effect, by economies of scale in leisure time and in work time, and by other economic factors.

3. Average hours worked for pay per employee have come to be a spurious indicator of hours of leisure per employee, as housewives and students enter the labor force. Hence, for recent years a series of hours worked per non-student male was computed.

4. While it is possible to see the influence of wage rates and unemployment on hours of work (and possibly of some secondary factors – e.g., education, recreation, fatigue – discussed in Chapter 2) it seems obvious that these factors are usually mediated by the political and legal environment. Thus, while the economic determinist might claim that such developments in hours determination as the establishment by the federal government of the N.R.A. or the acceptance by the Supreme Court of the F.L.S.A. were effects of the depression of the thirties, certainly the timing and the extent of governmental interference in the labor market in that period were conditioned by the political climate in Washington and by the legal traditions of the Court.

5. There has been a slowdown in hours reduction in the past thirty years.

The text table below shows that while there has been considerable reduction in hours of work in the past sixty years, the rate of decline has slowed down in recent decades. This conclusion holds even if hours are adjusted for the increases in vacations and holidays that have taken place since 1940.

	Hours of work per week		Real hourly wages	Relative price of recreation
1901	58.4		46.3	121.9
1929	48.7		83.2	96.9
1956	42.9 [44]	(41.9 [45])	184.3	92.0

44. Not adjusted for vacations and holidays.
45. Adjusted for vacations and holidays.

This slowdown is not due to a deceleration in the rate of wage gain. On the contrary, wages have risen more rapidly in the second than in the first period. Apparently it is not due to changes in unemployment, since the years selected here are years of relatively full employment.

A possible explanation is given in column 3 of the text table above. These data are from Table 4-B, and show changes in the price of commercial recreation relative to the general consumer price index. Recreation prices dropped in the first period, then remained relatively stable in the second. The possible association between the behavior of recreation and the movement in leisure time is pursued in Chapter 4 and in the following chapter.

3.7 SOURCES OF HOURS DATA

Hours Worked per Week

Hours worked per week per wage and salary earner in private, non-agricultural employment were estimated annually from 1900 to 1961.

The basic source for the 1951 to 1961 period is the monthly survey of the labor force conducted by the United States Bureau of the Census. The relative merits of using these interview data, rather than establishment or payroll data, have been discussed elsewhere [46] and need not concern us here. Essentially, establishment data yield hours per job, while interview data yield hours per employed person. For the purpose of a study of leisure the latter would seem to be the correct measure.

A breakdown of hours worked by wage and salary earners and by the self-employed and others has been available since 1958. The wage and salary sector has been divided into government and private subsectors since 1960. As the private wage and salary group has made up a rather stable proportion of the non-agricultural labor force over the last twenty years, the ratio of their hours to those of the non-agricultural labor force prevailing in recent years, about .97, was used for the post-1940 period.

Weekly hours data for the 1900 to 1940 period are based on unpublished materials on employment and man hours of wage and salary

---

46. KENDRICK, *Productivity Trends in the U.S.*; JONES, 'Hours of Work in the U.S., 1900-1957'; FINEGAN, 'Hours of Work in the U.S., A Cross-Sectional Analysis'; BRY, *The Average Workweek as an Economic Indicator*.

employees (excluding farm and general government) supplied to the author by John F. Kendrick. These data were linked to the survey-based data in 1941. Kendrick's materials were prepared for his recent book, *Productivity Trends in the United States.*

These data have the advantage of attempting to measure hours throughout the entire economy. A growing number of serious studies are available which analyze labor input and compute average hours worked in one industry or sector of the economy. Kendrick has pioneered in his careful sifting and weighting of the evidence to arrive at estimates of average hours worked for the entire economy.

Kendrick's data are based on establishment data, and reflect, in some cases, hours paid for rather than hours worked. However, multiple jobholding and paid leisure have become much more significant in the post-1940 period. Thus, it is hoped that movements in the Kendrick data are reasonably accurate estimates of time worked per person in the 1900 to 1940 period.[47]

Vacations and Holidays

Weekly hours data were adjusted to incorporate the effect of vacations and holidays on aggregate leisure (weekly basis).

Monthly and annual data on vacations taken by members of the labor force have been available since 1947. Since 1958, vacation data have been available for wage and salary workers in non-agricultural industries. On the basis of the labor force estimate of average vacation time for employed members of the labor force, non-agricultural wage and salary worker estimates were taken back to 1947. The estimates were then extrapolated back to 1941.[48]

These adjustments were refined with the help of Peter Henle's measures of the underestimation of vacation time in the government statistics.[49] This refinement led to an upward revision of the adjustment factor by one-fifth.[50]

47. Kendrick's data in the years 1929-1940 *et seq.* were adjusted by him to obtain hours per full-time equivalent employee. These were converted back to hours per full- and part-time employee. See OWEN, 'The Supply of Labor', pp. 194-97.
48. The percentage on vacation was extrapolated from 1947 to 1939 as an arithmetic progression equal to zero in 1939.
49. *Monthly Labor Review*, LXXXV (1962).
50. OWEN, 'The Supply of Labor', pp. 198-202. The vacation and holiday adjustment mechanisms are discussed at greater length in these pages.

78

Elimination of Females and Students from the Hours Data

Average hours worked per week for males and females in non-agricultural employment are available from the survey data from May, 1956, to date.[51] The censuses of 1940 and 1950 also give hours data by sex.

The male-female hours differential was computed for 1940, for 1950, and for 1956. The differential was then interpolated linearly for intervening years. This differential, in conjunction with annual statistics on male and female employment, permitted estimates of the male work week.

Employment statistics are available for male students by age group in the 1940 to 1960 period for all years except 1941 to 1943 and 1945. Average weekly hours data were published for working students in 1959 and 1960. Frequency distributions are available for earlier years, but class intervals were changed frequently, so that it is difficult to compute a time series of hours.[52]

Since the hours data are rough, fixed hours weights were used for each age class, thus making the implicit assumption that average hours in each age class were constant. However, the fact that the average age of employed students has declined and that the younger students work fewer hours a week reduced this measure of the average male student work week by about 10 percent over the twenty-year period.

51. The data were adjusted to eliminate non-wage and salary workers.
52. Such a series would probably show a declining movement in hours worked per student. One would expect this on *a priori* grounds, since reporting of short-hours personnel has become more accurate over the years.

CHAPTER 4

COMMERCIAL RECREATION IN THE UNITED STATES:

1900-1961

4.1 INTRODUCTION

In this chapter the quantity and price history of a segment of commercial or market recreation in the United States since 1900 is set forth. In Chapter 5, the data developed in this chapter are subjected to regression and correlation analyses. The reader who is more interested in these statistical results may move directly to Chapter 5.

4.2 COMMERCIAL RECREATION AND LEISURE TIME

One purpose of this study, suggested in Chapter 2, is to explore the possible relationship between leisure or non-working time and market goods and services consumed together with non-working time. In particular, it is interesting to analyze the relationship over time of hours of work and leisure to recreation demand and prices in the United States. Thus, one wants to analyze price changes and other developments in the recreation industry to explain changes in the labor market, and also to study changes in recreation demand to see how it might be affected by developments in the labor market.

The consumption of commercial recreation is, of course, restricted by definition to that portion of non-working time which is 'leisure' in the narrow sense. For a complete analysis of consumption time, sleeping, eating, and the like might be considered. Like recreation, these activities use non-working time and also use economic resources other than time. These resources might be priced and, for example, the prices used to test for complementarity with non-working time. However, as a first step in the analysis of non-working time, commercial recreation is an activity which seems likely to be complementary with non-working time and which is relatively simple to measure.

The United States Department of Commerce series on recreation expenditures (from the personal consumption component of the gross national product accounts) was used as a conceptual measure of commercial recreation. The Commerce Department collects expenditure data on, among others, the following recreation goods and services:

Books and maps; newspapers, magazines, and sheet music; games; toys, sporting, athletic, and photographic goods, boats and pleasure aircraft; radio and television receivers; records and musical instruments; radio and television repair; flowers, seeds, and potted plants; admissions to motion picture and legitimate theaters, operas, concerts, entertainments of non-profit organizations; admissions to professional baseball, football, and hockey games; admissions to horse and dog race tracks, college football, and other amateur spectator sports; payments – net of cash benefits – to fraternal, patriotic, and women's organizations exclusive of insurance; dues and fees af athletic, social, and luncheon clubs and school fraternities; dues and fees of billiard parlors, bowling alleys, dancing, riding, shooting, skating, and swimming places, amusement devices and parks; daily fee caddy fees; fees for sightseeing buses and guides and private flying instructions; photographic developing and printing, photo studios; collectors' net acquisitions of coins and stamps; hunting dog purchase and training, sports guide services, veterinarian services, purchase of pets; camp fees; and nonvending commercial machine receipts minus payoffs.[1]

One might say that these goods and services are purchased largely (though certainly not exclusively) for the purpose of 'refreshment of the strength and spirit after toil: diversion; play', and thus conform to Webster's definition of recreation. Moreover, sociological evidence supports the view that in the United States these activities do take up a large portion of what is conventionally regarded as leisure time.

The results of one of the most famous time analyses, *Leisure, A Suburban Study*, by Komarovsky, Lundberg, and McInerny (1934),[2] are summarized below in Table 4-A. This study was carried out in the early nineteen thirties in New York's Westchester County. Another time study, dating from the nineteen fifties, is summarized in Table

1. U.S., Department of Commerce, *U.S. Income and Output, A Supplement to the Survey of Current Business*, pp. 150, 152.
2. M. KOMAROVSKY, G.A. LUNDBERG, and M.A. MCINERNY, *Leisure, A Suburban Study* (N.Y.: Columbia University Press, 1934).

TABLE 4-A EMPIRICAL TIME BUDGET STUDIES

4-A-1: The Westchestet time budget study: hours per week spent in various activities

Activity	Laborers		White-collar workers		Professionals and executives		Unemployed		House-wives
	Male	Female	Male	Female	Male	Female	Male	Female	
Paid work	41.3	46.9	44.8	41.3	43.4		15.4	7.0	0.7
Transportation	5.6	7.0	5.6	7.7	8.4		3.5	4.9	5.6
Care of household and children	4.2	9.8	3.5	8.4	6.3		11.9	28.7	29.4
Personal care	5.6	7.0	4.9	7.0	4.9		4.9	7.0	7.0
Sleep	63.0	58.1	58.1	57.4	57.4		63.7	62.3	60.2
Eating	11.8	12.7	13.3	13.5	12.4		12.7	13.9	12.4
Visiting friends	11.0	8.6	9.5	11.0	9.2		13.0	16.1	17.6
Reading	11.0	4.4	7.1	5.0	8.6		14.9	9.1	9.8
Sports	4.1	2.3	4.0	2.2	4.7		7.8	2.8	1.9
Clubs	0	0	0.9	0.4	1.2		0.6	0.8	7.1
Radio	3.7	5.3	4.0	2.1	2.6		6.1	3.6	3.4
Motoring	1.4	1.5	2.3	2.9	1.8		1.8	2.2	1.2
Entertainment	4.1	3.4	5.3	5.6	1.8		3.3	5.0	5.1
Miscellaneous	0.6	0.9	4.1	3.9	4.7		4.3	4.9	5.8

Notes: 'Visiting' includes dancing and card-playing, etc., when done in a private house, as well as any meals with guests. 'Sports' includes participant sports only. 'Radio' excludes all radio listening done while doing something else, including other recreation (e.g., radio listening while reading goes under 'reading') – otherwise, the 'radio' category might be tripled.

Source: Komarovsky, Lundberg, and McInerny, *Leisure, A Suburban Study.*

4-A-2: The De Grazia time budget study: hours between 6 A.M. and 11 P.M. devoted to various activities

Activity	Age: 20-49 years		Age: 50 years or older	
	Male	Female	Male	Female
'Work'				
At work or school	5.9	1.6	4.5	1.0
Household chores	0.2	2.8	0.3	2.5
Miscellaneous work at home	0.7	1.1	0.9	1.2
Shopping	0.1	0.4	0.2	0.3
Traveling	1.5	0.7	0.8	0.5
Dressing, bathing, etc.	0.6	0.9	0.6	0.7
Preparing food *	0.0	1.3	0.0	0.9
Total 'Work'	9.0	8.8	7.3	7.1
'Leisure'				
Leisure	2.9	3.3	3.9	4.0
Visiting	0.7	1.0	0.5	0.7
Reading	0.8	0.7	1.3	1.4
Sleeping	2.1	1.9	2.4	2.3
At restaurant, tavern, bar, etc.	0.3	0.1	0.2	0.1
Eating *	1.2	1.2	1.4	1.4
Total 'Leisure'	8.0	8.2	9.7	9.9

Note: Some of these categories contain elements of work and of leisure, e.g., 'traveling' includes some pleasure driving.

* Category was 'eating and preparing food.' I took the liberty of dividing it on the following principles: 1. the Westchester study showed time spent in eating to be approximately equal for men and women; 2. I assumed that males spent no time preparing food.

Source: Sebastian De Grazia, 'The Uses of Time', R. W. Kleemeier (ed.), *Aging and Leisure* (N.Y.: Oxford University Press, 1961), pp. 113-54, especially Table 5.5, pp. 123-25. Source of time budget data presented by De Grazia is given as: 'Derived for use in the forthcoming Twentieth Century Fund Study of *Time, Work and Leisure,* from unpublished data collected for *A Nationwide Study of Living Habits,* a national survey conducted for the Mutual Broadcasting System by J. A. Ward.' De Grazia is the author of the Twentieth Century Fund Study.

4-B.[3] Both show that leisure time and market recreation are used simultaneously. Further evidence of the time intensity of market recreation activities may be found in the Y.W.C.A. study, *Leisure-Time Interests and Activities of Business Girls;*[4] the National Recreation Association's *Leisure Hours of 5,000 People;*[5] R. C. White's 'Social Class Differences in the Use of Leisure';[6] and A. C. Clarke's 'Leisure and Occupational Prestige'.[7]

4.3 AGGREGATE COMMERCIAL RECREATION: EXPENDITURES AND PRICES, 1900-1961

The demand for commercial recreation, whether measured by expenditures or in constant dollars, has grown more rapidly than the national economy in the 1900 to 1961 period. A period of very rapid relative growth took place from 1909 to 1929, when recreational spending as a percentage of total expenditures rose from 3.2 to 4.7 percent. Within the 1929 to 1961 period, recreation tended to follow the movements in total consumption fairly closely.

The price data in Table 4-B indicate that the expenditure estimates understate the growth of commercial recreation relative to other goods in the 1901 to 1929 period, since recreation prices relative to cost of living indexes dropped by 20 percent in those years. This is brought out in Table 4-C which shows the rapid increase in expenditures that one sees when the data are given in constant dollars.

As can be seen in the price series in Table 4-B, this decline in prices was not steady throughout the period. Relative prices of recreation goods dropped from 1901 through 1929, then showed virtually no *net* change in the following thirty years.

The index of relative prices of recreation goods is not very sensitive

3. Sebastian DE GRAZIA, 'The Uses of Time', in *Aging and Leisure*, edited by R.W. Kleemeier (N.Y.: Oxford University Press, 1961). See note to Table 4-A-2.

4. Young Women's Christian Association. *Leisure-Time Interests and Activities of Business Girls* (N.Y.: Women's Press, 1934).

5. National Recreation Association. *The Leisure Hours of 5,000 People* (N.Y.: National Recreation Association, 1934).

6. R.C.WHITE, 'Social Class Differences in the Use of Leisure', *American Journal of Sociology*, LXI (1955), 145-50.

7. A.C.CLARKE, 'Leisure and Occupational Prestige', *American Sociological Review*, XXI (June, 1956), 301-07.

TABLE 4-B
Recreation prices, 1901-1961

Year	Index of recreation prices	Index of relative recreation prices
	(1)	(2)
	(1949 = 100)	(1949 = 100)
1901	43.7	121.9
1906	45.9	121.0
1913	38.6	92.5
1919	70.9	97.6
1923	74.3	103.8
1926	71.6	96.4
1929	69.7	96.9
1930	63.6	90.8
1931	56.2	88.0
1932	51.3	89.4
1933	48.2	88.8
1934	45.7	81.3
1935	46.2	80.1
1936	46.0	78.9
1937	47.4	78.7
1938	48.2	81.4
1939	47.6	81.6
1940	49.2	83.6
1941	50.2	81.2
1942	53.0	77.5
1946	69.7	85.1
1947	81.9	87.3
1948	97.5	96.6
1949	100.0	100.0
1950	99.4	98.4
1951	104.5	95.9
1952	103.5	92.9
1953	105.0	93.4
1954	103.9	92.2
1955	103.5	92.0
1956	105.0	92.0
1957	109.0	92.4
1958	113.3	93.5
1959	115.2	94.2
1960	118.0	95.0
1961	120.6	96.0

Sources: see pp. 93-95 below.

to the business cycle. Relative prices of recreational goods and services did drop after the 1929 crash, falling to 83 percent of the 1929 level by 1935. But on closer analysis this price decline is associated with the dramatic changes in radio production and distribution that were taking place in this period.[8] If radios were excluded from the index, one would see rising relative prices for recreation goods and services in the 1929 to 1935 period.

TABLE 4-C

Per capita demand for recreation, 1901-1961

Year	Constant dollars	Year	Constant dollars
1901	18.1	1941	62.1
1906	21.8	1942	64.2
1913	30.3	1946	85.9
1919	30.5	1947	77.8
1923	32.9	1948	67.4
1926	39.0	1949	66.6
1929	50.1	1950	73.5
1930	50.0	1951	71.2
1931	46.5	1952	74.1
1932	37.5	1953	75.6
1933	35.7	1954	77.1
1934	41.5	1955	81.6
1935	43.9	1956	84.5
1936	50.3	1957	84.7
1937	54.3	1958	83.6
1938	50.8	1959	88.5
1939	54.3	1960	89.7
1940	56.8	1961	91.5

Sources: see pp. 93-95 below.

8. See pp. 88-89 below.

4.4 THE DEVELOPMENT OF THE MAJOR COMMERCIAL RECREATION INDUSTRIES, 1900-1961

Sporting Goods and Play Equipment

Perhaps the most steady gain over the last sixty years among commercial recreation industries, though certainly not the most highly publicized, has been in the sale of sporting goods and play equipment. This industry grew more rapidly than the recreation average in the 1900 to 1929 period, then doubled its share of the recreation budget in the thirty years that followed, rising from one-eighth in 1929 to one-quarter in 1961. Prices in this industry declined by about one-third relative to cost of living indexes in the 1901 to 1929 years but showed little net change in the more recent period.[9]

In contrast to the radio, television, or motion picture industries, sporting goods would seem to have been relatively unaffected by the new technology of the twentieth century. A closer examination of the products of this industry shows that this may not be the case. For example, technical advances in outdoor equipment made by the armed forces have been passed on to consumers and have been important in expanding the demand for sporting goods.[10]

While a portion of this play equipment is used by children, and while without doubt part of the growth in expenditures represents a switch from homemade to commercially-manufactured equipment, the record of rapid growth in sporting goods is consistent with the hypothesis that the increase in leisure activity has brought with it an increasing emphasis on leisure pursuits requiring physical activity.

Phonographs, Records, Radios, and Television Sets

Phonographs, records, radios, and television sets are considered here as one subdivision of the recreation industry. Each is an electrical appliance, used during leisure hours in the home to reproduce sights

---

9. Sources of price estimates of recreation are given in section 4.6 of this chapter. They are discussed in greater detail in OWEN, 'The Supply of Labor', Chapter VII.
10. J.F.DEWHURST and F.KLAFTER, 'Recreation', in *America's Needs and Resources, A New Survey*, edited by J. F. Dewhurst and associates (N.Y.: Twentieth Century Fund, 1955), pp. 346-77.

and/or sounds. The industries in this category have each experienced major technological changes which have drastically improved the quality of their products. These changes, in general, have been associated with declining relative prices.

The first of these to develop was, of course, the phonograph and record industry. By 1919 this industry, which was rather small in 1899, had grown to over sixty times its former size. Phonograph production dropped sharply in the next decade; by 1929 the value of production had dropped to about one-half that of 1919.[11] Record production only leveled off, presumably reflecting the durability of phonographs as opposed to the shorter life span of records.

A study of phonograph prices published in the Sears, Roebuck catalogues revealed little net change (less than 10 percent) in the relative price of phonographs in the 1901 to 1929 period. This long-term price stability was maintained despite numerous and significant improvements in phonograph equipment. The price history of the record industry is similar to what one would expect to find in a new and rapidly growing industry, since prices declined to about one-fourth of their 1901 value by 1929.

The decline of the phonograph and record industry in the nineteen twenties was more than offset by the rise of the radio. Sales of radio sets and tubes, insignificant in 1919, rose eightfold from 1923 to 1929. By 1929 radio sales were almost double the 1919 peak in record and phonograph sales.

The crash of 1929 seemed to bring a quick end to the boom in radio sales. Sales of radios and phonographs dropped by 75 percent from 1929 to 1931.[12] Production data indicate a decline in the output of radio sets from 4.4 million in 1929 to a low of 2.4 million in 1932.[13]

Figures showing declines in the dollar value of radio sales in the early thirties give an exaggerated picture of the true decline in the demand for new radios that took place. Information collected on the radio industry from 1929 on indicates that the period of the early thirties was one of significant technical improvement and of drastic price reduction. But even if sales data are corrected for price changes,

11. U.S., Department of Commerce, Bureau of the Census, *Census of Manufactures*, 1899-1929.
12. W.H.LOUGH, *High Level Consumption* (N.Y.: McGraw-Hill Book Co., Inc., 1935).
13. U.S., Department of Commerce, *Historical Statistics of the United States, Colonial Times to 1957*, p. 491.

a very poor picture of the demand for radios in this period is still obtained. While production data show a sharp drop in set production from 1929 to 1932, followed by a recovery to the 1929 level by 1934,[14] data on the number of families with radios show [14] that the number of radio families continued to rise throughout the nineteen thirties.[15] Thus, these figures would seem to indicate that while purchases declined, total demand for radios, including used radios, increased throughout the depression.[16]

The next important technical innovation in this area was, of course, the introduction of television. While some sets were installed before World War II, the boom in sales of television sets came in the late nineteen forties. By 1950, 12 percent of homes in the United States had television sets; by 1955, the figure was 67 percent, and by 1960, 88 percent.[17]

These gains in the television industry were probably stimulated by price reductions. The relative price of television sets showed a decline of almost one-third from December, 1950, to December, 1955. Moreover, while these price reductions measure, though imperfectly, changes in the quality of television sets, they do not reflect the improvements in programming that may have been achieved during those years.

While the average quality of individual shows may not have improved much, there was an increase in the number of hours during the day in which programs were offered and, because of the proliferation of channels, in the choice of programs. Thus, there is an upward bias in this price series.

Motion Pictures

Admissions expenditures rose sixtold from 1919 to 1929. The U. S.

14. *Ibid.*, p. 491.
15. The large increase in radio sets in use was not at all typical of the behavior of other consumer durables in the 1929 to 1933 period. The number of automobiles registered and telephones in use declined in this period.
16. As measured by sets in use. However, the increased age of sets in use in this period indicated by this analysis would point to a 'quality' deterioration that would tend to reduce the value of sets in use. The quality of sets sold was also changing, as a trend towards the purchase of table models, rather than consoles, was offset by technical improvements in the sets themselves.
17. U.S., Department of Commerce, Bureau of the Census, *Statistical Abstract of the United States;* 1953 edition, p. 776 and 1961 edition, p. 821.

study of consumer budgets in 1918 showed that three-quarters of admissions paid were for motion pictures. By 1934-1936 the proportion rose to nine-tenths.[18] Thus the gain in admissions is very largely the story of the growth of the motion picture industry.

The first motion picture theater was the Nickelodeon, which opened on June 19, 1905.[19] The industry grew rapidly, and theaters opened in city after city.[20] One writer estimates average weekly attendance at motion pictures in the United States in 1910 at 10 million.[21] Trade sources estimate weekly attendance at 50 million by 1926.[22] While the attendance statistics are decidedly weak, the budget study estimate of 1918 mentioned above and the federal admissions tax figures for World War I show that the movies were dominating the commercial entertainment industry just thirteen years after the opening of the Nickelodeon.[23]

Quality biases in the motion picture admissions series are much more serious than those in the radio, phonograph, and television price indexes. Important changes were made in the quality of the motion picture throughout its history. Shows tended to be longer, and the technical quality of the film was improved. The most dramatic of these changes was the introduction of sound in 1927. By 1936, over 90 percent of the motion picture houses in the country were equipped to reproduce sound.[24]

Unfortunately, data on admissions charges do not record any of these improvements. The relative price of admissions rose by over 26 percent in the years from 1913 through 1929 and had risen by 46 percent by 1939. Since no attempt was made at the time to allow for improvements in the quality of motion pictures (it would have been a most difficult task), it is obvious that the admissions charge component of the recreation price index has an upward bias.

Admissions were not hit too badly by the depression: revenue declined by 37 percent from 1929 to 1933, then gained steadily during

18. U.S., Bureau of Labor Statistics, *Bulletin*, Nos. 357 and 638.

19. *Motion Picture Herald*, July 29, 1939, p. 15.

20. *Moving Picture World* (a trade magazine for motion picture exhibitors), 1906-1910. Various issues.

21. DEWHURST and KLAFTER, 'Recreation', p. 356.

22. *Film Daily Yearbook, 1954 Edition* (N.Y.: The Film Daily, 1954).

23. See LOUGH, *High Level Consumption*, p. 277.

24. Julius WEINBERGER, 'The Economic Aspects of Recreation', *Harvard Business Review*, XVI (No. 4, 1937), p. 453.

the later depression years and the war.[25] Motion picture attendance hit its peak in 1946, when there were 81 million admissions per week.

Commercial entertainment did not participate in the postwar boom. Admissions charges dropped from one-quarter of recreational expenditures in 1948 [26] to one-tenth in 1960.[27] While competition from the television industry is usually regarded as the prime cause of the depression in admissions, this decline was probably accentuated by a 14 percent rise in the relative price of motion pictures in the 1948 to 1958 period.

Newspapers, Magazines, and Books

After a period of rapid growth in the nineteenth century, by 1900 newspapers, magazines, and books had a dominant position in the commercial recreation industry. The percentage of the recreation budget spent on reading declined in the next thirty years as the newer forms of commercial recreation became established. However, reading expenditures in the 1900 to 1929 years did grow at about the same rate as the national income.[28] In 1961 the share of reading in recreation expenditures was at about the 1929 level of one-fifth.[29]

Virtually no net change in the relative price of reading matter occurred over the 1900 to 1961 period. Like the admission charge series, newsstand and subscription prices of a periodical do not reflect quality changes. Thus there is a possibility of an upward or a downward bias in the price series. However, the quality changes that have taken place in newspapers, magazines, and books in the past sixty years have been of a less dramatic nature than those in motion pictures.

Musical Instruments

The musical instrument was a more important component of the rec-

25. U.S., Department of Commerce, *National Income 1929-1953, A Supplement to the Survey of Current Business*.
26. U.S., Department of Commerce, *Survey of Current Business*, July, 1961.
27. U.S., Department of Commerce, *U.S. Income and Output*.
28. U.S., Department of Commerce, Bureau of the Census, *Census of Manufactures* 1899-1929; and W. H. LOUGH, *High Level Consumption* (N.Y.: McGraw-Hill Book Co., Inc., 1935).
29. U.S., Department of Commerce, *National Income 1929-1953, A Supplement to the Survey of Current Business;* and *Survey of Current Business*, July, 1961.

reation industry in the 1900 to 1930 period than in later years. While the dollar value of musical instrument production did rise in these early years, their share of total recreation manufacturing declined drastically, from one-quarter to one-sixteenth.[30] The rate of growth in musical instruments was far below that of national income.

Pianos dominated musical instrument production throughout the three decades, amounting to about 50 percent of total industry values. When musical instrument production collapsed in the later nineteen twenties, about 70 percent of the decline was in pianos. Part of the explanation of this drop may be found in the decline of the player piano as American consumers turned to more sophisticated forms of musical reproduction.[31]

4.5 CONCLUSIONS

The commercial recreation industry has grown very rapidly in the twentieth century. This growth in aggregate recreation took place in spite of obsolescence and stagnation in several of the component commercial recreation industries.

While growth occurred throughout the last sixty years, the relative growth rate was somewhat greater before 1929 than it has been since then. Moreover, all the reduction in the relative price of recreation took place in the early period. This parallels the movements in the hours of leisure series (see pp. 76-77), which grew somewhat more rapidly in the 1900 to 1929 period than in the next thirty years.

Shorter run movements in leisure and recreation display no such parallelism. Employee leisure time was abundant in the nineteen thirties, but recreation sales plummeted at the same rate as other consumption. This disparity may have had a number of causes. The leisure time series is derived from employees only; leisure time of the self-employed may not have increased in the thirties. Moreover, those employees put on short time by their employers may have been toward the bottom of the income distribution and thus may have had relatively little effect on aggregate demand for commercial recreation.

30. U.S., Department of Commerce, Bureau of the Census, *Census of Manufactures*, 1923-1929.
31. Production of pianos with player attachments declined by over 70 percent from 1923 to 1929.

Again, this divergence may have been accentuated by the fact that current sales of recreation goods were a poor indicator of total recreation demand in the nineteen thirties, since the stocks of many durable recreation goods in use were relatively new.

Returning to the longer run analysis, it was shown that the price of recreation series is also biased, since the motion picture and the newspapers and magazines series do not incorporate any quality changes, and the radio and television series only attempt to measure changes in the quality of the sets, not in the extent and quality of programming. Nevertheless, there does seem to be some empirical relationship between declines in the relative price of recreation and the rate of increase in the hours of leisure series.

Regression and correlation techniques are used to explore these various relationships further in the following chapter.

4.6 SOURCES OF RECREATION DATA

Annual estimates of expenditures for commercial recreation, beginning with 1929, are available from the Department of Commerce. Data on the recreation industry for earlier years are rather sparse, since most of the pioneers in national income and product statistics did not assemble price or production data for the recreation industry.

Expenditure data for recreation products for the 1909 to 1929 period are taken from William Lough's *High Level Consumption*,[32] which does make such estimates. The estimates of expenditures on recreation services for 1909 to 1929 are based on Julius Weinberger's 'The Economic Aspects of Recreation'.[33] The resulting Lough-Weinberger series was then linked to the Department of Commerce data at 1929. Census of Manufactures data on recreation manufactures were employed to estimate the 1900 to 1909 movement in recreation expenditures.[34]

32. W. H. LOUGH, *High Level Consumption* (N.Y.: McGraw-Hill Book Co., Inc., 1935).
33. Julius WEINBERGER, 'The Economic Aspects of Recreation', *Harvard Business Review*, XVI (No. 4, 1937), 448-63.
34. Estimates for intercensal years were made by linear interpolation.

TABLE 4-D

Recreation in the budget studies of 1918, 1934-1936, and 1950

Recreation expenditure per type as percentage of total

Year	Play equipment	Radios, TV, phonographs	Records	Sheet music	Musical instruments	Cameras and supplies	Newspapers, magazines, and books	Admissions	Club dues	Other	Total recreation spending
1918	9.5	6.5	2.8	5.2	11.6		20.9	20.4	6.5	17.0	100
1934-36	4.2	9.1	0.3		2.1	1.1	28.8	34.9	3.7	15.7	100
1950	9.5	25.4		1.7	2.5	2.9	16.8	20.5	4.1	16.6	100

Sources: 1918, U.S., Bureau of Labor Statistics, *Bulletin*, No. 357; 1934-36, *Bulletin*, No. 638; 1950, Special tabulation of 1950 Budget Study by Arnold E. Chase (letter to writer, March 30, 1961), Division of Prices and Cost of Living, U.S., Bureau of Labor Statistics, Department of Labor.

Information on the history of recreation prices in the United States is even more limited than expenditure data. Price indexes of motion picture admission charges and of newspaper prices have been published by the Bureau of Labor Statistics as part of its Consumer Price Index since 1935. Radio sets were added in September, 1949, television sets, in December, 1950, and television repairs and toys and sporting goods, in December, 1952. Another source of data is the Department of Commerce's Wholesale Price Index, which gives prices of radios, toys, and sporting goods for the 1948 to 1953 period. Thus, if one is willing to overlook changes in retail margins, it is possible to extend almost all of the C.P.I. recreation component back to 1948.

A third source is the National Industrial Conference Board, which collected price data on newspapers and magazines and on motion pictures on a monthly basis from 1920. The N.I.C.B. also obtained price quotes on these items in 1914 and in 1918.

In order to obtain estimates of prices of recreation goods other than reading matter or admissions prior to 1948, Sears, Roebuck and Company catalogues were employed, and prices of a number of recreation goods were obtained and aggregated into the following categories: play and sporting equipment; radios, television sets, and phonographs; records; cameras; musical instruments, and, for the 1901 to 1929 period, sheet music. These categories were suggested by the several Bureau of Labor Statistics studies. Recreational items which were of some importance in the consumer budget,[35] and which could be priced by means of the mail order catalogue, were obtained.

Admission prices were calculated from newspaper advertisements for movies and other entertainments. The other entertainment group included vaudeville and burlesque shows, spectacles, and musical programs. An index of newspaper prices was obtained in part from contemporary editions of N. W. Ayer and Sons' *Directory of Newspapers and Periodicals*. These data were linked with the N.I.C.B. series to obtain indexes of admissions and reading prices. This series was then linked with the B.L.S. admissions and reading indexes at 1935.

These several recreation price series were then weighted in accordance with their relative weight in the three budget studies (the 1918 study for the years 1901 to 1929; the 1934-1936 study for the 1929 to 1942 period; and the 1950 study for 1942 to 1948) to obtain an index of recreation prices for 1900 to 1948. This index was linked at 1948 to the extended recreation component of the Consumer Price Index.[36]

The recreation quantity series was obtained by dividing the expenditure data by this price series. An index of the relative price of recreation was calculated by dividing the recreation price index by a cost of living index. Price deflators were obtained by linking Albert Rees' cost of living index [37] with the U.S. Bureau of Labor Statistics Consumer Price Index in 1913.

---

35. However, the notion of what is commercial recreation was the one which is now used by the U.S. Department of Commerce rather than that employed in contemporary budget studies. Thus, tobacco was not considered to be a portion of recreation in the nineteen thirties, even though the budget study of 1934-1936 classified it as such. Again, the 1918 budget study recreation classification was made more comparable to current notions by adding musical instruments, talking machines, cameras, dues, and reading. (See note to Table 4-D.)

36. Obtained by extending the C.P.I. with wholesale price quotes where necessary. See p. 94.

37. Albert REES, *Real Wages in Manufacturing, 1890-1914* (National Bureau of Economic Research General Series, No. 70. Princeton: Princeton University Press, 1961).

CHAPTER 5

EMPIRICAL MODELS AND SOME STATISTICAL RESULTS

The income-leisure and related choices are analyzed in this chapter by means of regression and correlation analyses of time series of American data for the period 1900 to 1961. The time series of annual leisure time developed in Chapter 3, and the data on the recreation industry presented in Chapter 4 provide a number of the relevant series.

The analytical notions developed in Chapter 1, and especially in Chapter 2, are drawn upon to provide the models used for empirical tests in the present chapter.[1] More specifically, an attempt is made to go beyond the conventional analysis, which explains time series of hours of work in terms of changes in the wage rate, in several ways:

First, by utilizing the relationship between recreation and leisure time. This is done in more than one way, including the use of the price of recreation as an explanatory variable in the analysis of the demand for leisure time, and, conversely, by the use of the price of leisure as an explanatory variable in the analysis of the demand for market recreation; the analysis of the demand for leisure activity (a composite of leisure time and market recreation); and the estimation of the elasticity of substitution between leisure time and market recreation.

Second, by analyzing the effects of unemployment on the price of leisure and hence on the demand for leisure time of employed (or partially employed) workers. This is done in three ways: by using the employment rate as an independent variable, by permitting the unemployment rate to affect the price of leisure, and by analyzing a subsample of years in which unemployment rates were quite low.

Third, by adding leisure time to the empirical measures of real income and of the price of leisure used as explanatory variables. The conventional measure of real income (money income divided by a

---

1. An exception is the employer labor demand model presented in sections 5.3 and 5.4. This model is based upon an adaptation of the Cobb-Douglas production function.

price index) reflects the choice of a level of leisure time and thus may not be suitable to use as an independent variable in the estimation of leisure time. Hence, in one set of regressions, real income is measured by adding leisure time to the conventional measure of income (and then by deflating this measure by a price index which includes the price of leisure).

Fourth, by introducing output-reducing fatigue as a determinant of the price of leisure. In several of the models worker income is permitted to rise at a decreasing rate as hours of work are increased beyond a certain level.

Fifth, the employer demand for labor model mentioned above is utilized to obtain estimates of the employee demand for leisure time that are independent of the biases inherent in single-equation estimates (e.g., those that would arise out of the dependence of the real wage rate on the supply of hours of work per worker).

Commuting, education, and working conditions were not utilized in the empirical work, despite their potential importance as determinants of the demand for leisure. Their omission was not due to any underestimation of the possible importance of these variables, but rather to the difficulties of obtaining the relevant data.[2]

Section 5.1 analyzes the demand for leisure time per worker of wage and salary employees in the United States in the 1900 to 1961 period. A model of employer demand for hours of work is developed in section 5.2. In section 5.3 a two-equation model is estimated which incorporates both the employee demand for leisure time and the employer demand for labor relationships.

Section 5.4, 'The Demand for Market Recreation', further examines the relationship between leisure time and market recreation by estimating the demand for market recreation as a function of real income, the relative price of leisure and the relative price of recreation. Section 5.5 then gives a statistical analysis of the demand for 'leisure activity', a composite of leisure time and market recreation, while section 5.6 analyzes the determination of the proportion in which leisure time and market recreation are used at a given level of leisure activity.

---

2. As the analyses of Chapter 2 showed, it would not be enough to obtain estimates of the amount of commuting or education, or the quality of working conditions. Rather, more sophisticated variables are called for which would measure the proliferation of commuting and educational opportunities, and the net cost to employers of providing good working conditions. Such data were not readily available.

Employee demand for leisure time in the United States, 1900-1961, is estimated empirically in this section. Time series used in this empirical work are discussed in sections 5.1.a-b (additional data series were discussed in Chapters 3 and 4). Empirical models are then presented in sections 5.1.c-f. Finally, regression and correlation results obtained from fitting these empirical models to the data are analyzed in sections 5.1.g-m.

a. Time Series of Wage Rates and Unemployment

Chapters 3 and 4 give estimates of hours of work and of the relative price of recreation. In order to estimate either labor income or the relative price of leisure variables needed for the employee demand for leisure time model, measures of the hourly wage rate and of unemployment are also needed.

Hourly compensation [3] of wage and salary employees in the private, non-farm sector of the U. S. economy, 1900 to 1960, are given in column 1 of Table 5-A. These data were subsequently divided by an index of consumer prices to obtain real compensation per hour. The deflated estimates are shown in column 2 of Table 5-A.

Average compensation per man hour was obtained for the years 1929 to 1960 by dividing the total employee compensation (net of farm and government) statistics published by the United States Department of Commerce [4] by John Kendrick's estimates of employee man hours in the private, non-farm sector. Kendrick designed his man hours series to be consistent with the Department of Commerce compensation estimates, and hence no further adjustment was made.

Man-hour compensation rates in the 1919 to 1929 period were obtained by using the compensation and employment data developed by

---

3. This includes various fringe benefits, as well as cash payments. See Albert REES, *New Measures of Wage Earner Compensation in Manufacturing, 1914-1957*, National Bureau of Economic Research Occasional Paper, No. 75 (N.Y.: National Bureau of Economic Research, 1960).

4. See U.S., Office of Business Economics, *National Income, A Supplement to the Survey of Current Business, 1954 Edition*, p. 59 and pp. 68-77, for a definition of the compensation measure used there.

TABLE 5-A

Average compensation per hour of private non-farm
employees in the United States

Year	Current dollars (dollars per hour)	1947-1949 dollars (dollars per hour)
1900	.157	.438
1910	.209	.512
1920	.568	.663
1930	.612	.857
1940	.663	1.107
1950	1.602	1.558
1960	2.536	2.000

Source: See text.

Simon Kuznets [5] together with the Kendrick employment and hours data. (The Kuznets data were used to obtain a compensation per employee index. This was then divided by an hours per employee series, based upon the Kendrick estimates, to obtain compensation per hour.)

For earlier years, Kendrick estimates of compensation per man hour for various non-manufacturing industries in 1899, 1909 and 1919 were combined with estimates of hourly compensation in manufacturing made by Albert Rees [6] to obtain compensation measures for these bench-mark years. Year-to-year movements in the compensation index in the 1899 to 1919 period were estimated by interpolation, using Rees' annual estimates for compensation in manufacturing.

Annual estimates of the unemployment rate – unemployment as a percentage of the civilian labor force – were made for the years 1900 to 1961. U. S. Bureau of Labor Statistics unemployment data were used in the post-1929 period.[7] Data for the years 1900 to 1929 were taken from S. Lebergott's study in the National Bureau of Economic Research volume, *The Measurement and Behavior of Unemployment.*[8]

5. Simon KUZNETS, *National Income and Its Composition, 1919-1938.*
6. Albert REES, *Real Wages in Manufacturing, 1890-1914;* and National Bureau of Economic Research, *The Measurement and Behavior of Unemployment.* See OWEN, 'The Supply of Labor', pp. 100-04 for a description of these sources.
7. Adjusted for changes in the Bureau of Labor Statistics definition of unemployment in 1957. See OWEN, *op.cit.*, pp. 104-05 for details.
8. See footnotes 5 and 6 above.

A major use to which these data were put was to select a series of full employment peak years which would make it possible to study the effects of economic variables on hours of work in circumstances in which the influence of unemployment disequilibria was minimized.[9] 'Full employment peak' years were selected by the following rules: 1. Unemployment should be less than 4.5 percent. 2. Years should not be closer than every third year, to avoid taking more than one observation per cycle. 3. In each such period of relatively full employment, the year of lowest unemployment was selected. 4. War years were excluded. These rules selected 1901, 1906, 1913, 1919, 1923, 1926, 1929, 1948, 1953, and 1956.

b. A Time Series of Leisure Time

Leisure hours per week of non-student male employees should be measured as $L = 168 - $ (male) household work hours $-$ hours of market employment.[10]

Thus, an accurate measure of leisure time would use data on male household work as well as hours of work statistics. But annual variations in hours of male household work are not available. Moreover, the several time budgets we have that purport to measure this variable do not suffice to establish any secular trend. Hence, an average figure was taken, 18 hours a week (based on the two time budgets shown in Table 4-A, pp. 82-83), and subtracted from 168 hours a week to obtain an estimate, 150 hours, of time spent in market work or in consumption.

9. At full employment labor income may be proportional to the wage rate. But, in the long run, this is only an approximation, since *permanent* income is influenced by periods of unemployment (see Milton FRIEDMAN, *A Theory of the Consumption Function*. National Bureau of Economic Research General Series, No. 63; Princeton: Princeton University Press, 1957). However, several experiments of ours which attempted to explain variations in leisure time by using alternative measures of permanent income did not prove fruitful.

10. This resulting leisure variable 'L' is of course an overestimate according to such writers as Aristotle, Pieper, and De Grazia.

However, the demand equations fitted in this chapter are linear in form. Those readers who believe that the concept of leisure should be reserved for consumption time net of some constant amount of time needed for sleeping, eating, and the like, and those readers (e.g., Aristotelians) who believe that the concept of recreation time should also be netted, may wish to subtract a constant from our measure 'L' to obtain a more

c. Empirical Measures of Real Income and the Price of Leisure in Full Employment Model

In many of the regressions that follow, the measures of real income and of the general price level include leisure time as a component. The reasons for including leisure are straightforward. If leisure time is a consumer 'good', then it should be evaluated in a measure of real income. There are at least two arguments in defense of this view: first, that the growth over time of real income is measured more realistically if it includes leisure time than if this very large component of economic well-being is excluded. Second, a more narrowly economic argument is that if real income is measured in the conventional manner (1) $Y = wH = w(K - L)$, i.e., as the real value of weekly money income, the measure of income is directly dependent upon the income-leisure choice which it is supposed to determine.

The simplest way to include leisure time in real income would be to price leisure time at the market rate (i.e., at the real hourly wage rate), and then to add it to conventional real income to obtain nominal real income: (2) $Y_n = wH + LP(L)$. If the price of leisure equals the wage rate, the equation (2) reduces to (3) $Y_n = w(H + L) = wK$, where K is a constant.

A critical defect in this simple measure lies in the implication that the value of leisure time rises with the real hourly wage rate,[11] whereas in fact the amount of leisure received may not. This objection may be met by the use of a somewhat more refined measure of real income. Here, one expands the index of prices used to deflate money income to include the price of leisure.

acceptable estimate. This may be done by reducing the value of 'a', the constant term in the linear regression.

But if the reader feels that the amount of consumption time spent in non-leisure activities is not constant but is rather changing over time, then such a simple transformation will not suffice. If these hours probably have in fact increased over time (due perhaps to an increase in commuting time) there may be an upward bias in the leisure data over time.

11. This may actually be true, either in a trivial or in a non-trivial sense. In the trivial case, it might be argued that, with a rising wage rate, the relative cost of leisure rises, and hence, in equilibrium the ratio of the marginal utility of leisure to that of goods and services rises. But this argument could be used to justify the inclusion of any good in real income at its current price. An obvious flaw in the argument is that the rise in the ratio of marginal utilities could as well be due to a decline in the marginal utility of goods and services as to an increase in the marginal utility of leisure.

In this model, the price of leisure is incorporated into the price index (P.I.) by regarding the conventional Consumer Price Index as being composed of $m = n - 1$ commodities. Then if leisure is the nth good, the Laspeyres index may be expanded as follows:

$$(4)\ \text{P.I.} = \frac{\sum_{i=1}^{n-1} p_i^1 \times_t^0 + p^1 (L) L^0}{\sum_{1=1}^{n-1} p_i^0 \times_i^0 + P^0 (L) L^0}$$

Equation (4) may be rewritten

$$(5)\ \text{P.I.} = c(\text{C.P.I.}) + (1 - c) \frac{P^1(L)}{P^0(L)}$$

where c equals the weight of non-leisure income in total income in the base period, and $1 - c$ equals the weight of leisure income. Equating the price of leisure to the wage rate at full employment and defining P.I.$'$ = P.I./C.P.I., then, in years of full employment P.I. $= \alpha + \beta w$, where α and β are constants and w is the conventionally defined real wage rate. The relative price of leisure $P(L)' = \dfrac{w}{\alpha + \beta w}$ and real income per employee = $\dfrac{wK}{\alpha + \beta w}$ where K is a constant equal to $H + L$.

Thus, in this full employment model, $Y' = KP(L)'$, where K is a constant. Since the two series must be in proportion, an index of the relative price of leisure is indistinguishable from an index of real income per employee. Column 5 of Table 5-B presents an index (w$'$) of real income per employee and of the relative price of leisure for ten peak employment years.

These adjustments yield an income measure whose rate of growth is much more modest than that indicated by the real hourly wage rate w (column 3) or that indicated by the more conventional measure of the real value of money income (H). Insofar as one wishes to measure the

A quite distinct, and non-trivial, argument is that the value of leisure time rises with economic development for the same reasons as that of an hour of work: increases in productivity (due in turn to more capital and especially to a better technology at the disposal of consumers). See p. 143 below for further discussion.

102

resources utilized by the consumer (goods and time), the measure w'
seems to be superior to the conventional one.[12]

TABLE 5-B

Empirical estimates of time series used in leisure time
supply model regression analysis

Year	Hours of work per week (H)	Hours of leisure per week (L)	Hourly wage rate per constant dollars W)	Relative price of recreation P(R)*	Index of income per employee or price of leisure (W')
	(1)	(2)	(3)	(4)	(5)
1901	58.4	91.6	45.0	121.9	84.7
1906	57.0	93.0	50.5	121.0	90.3
1913	55.0	95.0	54.6	92.5	94.1
1919	50.0	100.0	67.0	97.6	104.2
1923	49.6	100.4	77.0	103.8	110.8
1926	49.3	100.7	78.0	96.4	111.5
1929	48.7	101.3	83.2	96.9	114.6
1948	41.7	108.3	136.4	96.6	136.4
1953	41.5	108.5	163.6	93.4	143.6
1956	41.9	108.1	184.3	92.0	148.0

* Series used in regression equal to 100 in 1949.

Sources: H: Table 3-A; L: 150—H; W: See text; P(R): Table 4-B; w': $\dfrac{w}{\alpha + \beta w}$; see text.

d. An Empirical Model of Output-reducing Fatigue

It was argued in Chapter 2 that while a worker's output might be expected to rise more or less proportionately with his hours of work up
to some level of hours (say 35 to 48 per week), one could only expect
less than proportional gains in output beyond that level of hours. In the

12. If the end is to measure the value of the leisure activities carried on by consumers
and if consumer technology were improving, then this goods-time series might be
biased downward. But if the technological change is neutral between consumption
goods and services and consumption time, it is hard to see how it would affect the
demand for leisure-time formulations.

empirical work of the present chapter, 'fatigue functions' are introduced that assume that weekly labor income of employees rises in proportion to hours of work to some level of hours z, and then rises less than proportionately beyond that level.[13]

Several alternative estimates of income and the price of leisure were developed on the assumption that output-reducing fatigue is of a rather simple sort, such that the price of leisure, or the marginal contribution to labor income of an hour of work is equal to $\left(\dfrac{Z}{H}\right)^x w_0$, where x is some positive constant, when $H \geq Z$, and is equal to w_0 (i.e., the wage rate earned in the absence of fatigue) when $H < Z$. Thus, labor income $= w_0 H$ when $H \leq Z$; otherwise, $Y = w_0 F(H) =$

$$w_0 \left[\int_Z^h \left(\frac{Z}{H}\right)^x dH + z\right] = w_0 \left[\frac{z}{x-1}(x - (z/H)^{x-1})\right]$$

When $x = 1$, the integral is solved as: $Y = w_0 z \left(1 + \log \dfrac{H}{Z}\right)$. Since the conventional measure of the wage rate $\hat{w}$ equals average hourly earnings,

$$w_0 = \frac{\hat{w}H}{\dfrac{z}{x-1}(x - Z/H)} x - 1.$$

Estimates of w_0 based upon different values of x and z were computed and are shown in columns 3-7 of Table 5-C. If one of these fatigue relations is the correct one, then in 1900 average hourly compensation paid was less than the base, or fatigueless, wage, but by 1929 or 1948 much of the discrepancy was eliminated. That is, the increase in average hourly compensation ($\hat{w}$) overestimated the rate of increase in wage rates (w_0). Since then, average hourly earnings have mirrored movements in wages more closely.

Thus, the small acceleration in the rate of increase in wages that appears in an analysis of average hourly compensation becomes much greater when fatigue is posited. If a rather strong fatigue effect is assumed, with $z = 35$ and $x = 2$, the average annual rate of growth from 1901 to 1929 in the base, or fatigueless, wage is calculated at 1.8 percent. In the 1929-1956 period the calculated rate of growth in the base wage rate rises to 2.7 percent.

---

13. It is thus implicitly assumed that the twentieth century American worker has not been working hours at or beyond the level that maximizes output.

104

TABLE 5-C

Empirical measure of the fatigue effect:
full employment years: 1900-1961

Year	H	z x (no fatigue)	W_0 40 ½	40 2	40 3	35 2	35 3
1901	58.4	45.0	46.4	49.9	51.9	53.6	56.8
1906	57.0	50.5	51.8	55.4	57.4	59.3	62.7
1913	55.0	54.6	55.8	59.0	60.8	62.9	66.2
1919	50.0	67.0	67.7	69.8	71.0	73.6	76.2
1923	49.6	77.0	77.8	80.0	81.3	84.2	87.2
1926	49.3	78.0	78.8	80.9	82.1	85.2	88.0
1929	48.7	83.2	84.0	85.9	87.1	90.3	93.2
1948	41.7	136.4	136.9	136.5	136.8	140.0	141.6
1953	41.5	163.6	163.6	163.8	163.9	167.8	169.5
1956	41.9	184.3	184.5	184.7	184.9	189.4	191.8

Source: See text.

In order to examine the effects of using the different values of z and x, an empirical labor supply or demand for leisure time model was employed of the form (1) $H = aw_0^b P(L)^c P(R)^d$, where w_0 is a proxy variable for income. If $P(L) = w_0 \left(\dfrac{Z}{H}\right)^x$, then (1) may be rewritten as (2) $H = gw_0^r P(R)^s$, where $g = \left(az^{cx}\right)^{\frac{1}{1+cx}}$, $r = \dfrac{b+c}{1+cx}$, and $s = \dfrac{d}{1+cx}$.

e. Empirical Measures of Real Income and the Price of Leisure in Years of Less than Full Employment (Annual Variations Model)

Table 5-D gives wage, unemployment, and recreation price data for thirty years in the 1929 to 1961 period. The war years 1943 to 1945 were excluded because of the difficulty of obtaining meaningful price quotations in this period of rationing and shortages. But the remaining thirty years display a variety of economic conditions, ranging from prosperity to depression. These years were selected to facilitate the examination of the determination of hours of work and leisure under more typical, less than full employment conditions.

The introduction of these years of less than full employment requires a modification of the income and price of leisure measures introduced for the full employment years model.

Section 2.11, 'Unemployment and Hours of Work', showed that the employed worker, faced with a curtailment of hours demand by his employer, experiences a drop in real income and a somewhat greater drop in the price of leisure. This theory did not develop a way of estimating the quantitative relationship between unemployment and the price of leisure. However, it may be possible to estimate such a relationship with empirical data.

Using the simple hypothesis that the relative decline in the price of leisure is in a constant ratio to the relative decline in employment, write:

$$\frac{\text{Wage Rate} - \text{Price of Leisure}}{\text{Wage Rate}} = e \left(\frac{\text{Number Unemployed}}{\text{Labor Force}} \right)$$

where e is some constant. Solving for the price of leisure, $P(L) = W(1 - eU)$, where U is the unemployment rate.

One would expect e to be greater than zero (since one would not expect unemployment to *raise* the price of leisure). The price of leisure would be greater than zero, unless employees preferred work to income. Since the unemployment rate in 1933 was almost one-fourth, e would have to be less than or equal to four to avoid a negative price of leisure in that year. Thus, on the basis of the model $P(L) = W(1-eU)$, one would expect e to be in the range 0 to 4.0. In order to explore the implications of this model, forty values of e, ranging from 0 to 4.0, were selected, and a time series of the price of leisure was computed for each of these values.

But the true relationship between the wage rate and the price of leisure need not fit this linear model exactly. A closer *average* re-

106

TABLE 5-D

*Empirical estimates of time series used in leisure time supply
model regression analysis: annual data, 1929-1961*

Year	Hours of leisure per week L	Hours of work per week H	Real hourly wage rate W	Unemployment rate U(%)	Relative price of recreation P(R)
1929	101.3	48.7	83.2	3.2	96.9
1930	102.9	47.1	85.7	8.9	90.8
1931	104.4	45.6	90.5	15.9	88.0
1932	106.3	43.7	91.6	23.6	89.4
1933	106.7	43.3	91.3	24.9	88.8
1934	109.4	40.6	98.6	21.7	81.3
1935	108.3	41.7	98.3	20.1	80.1
1936	106.6	43.4	98.3	17.0	78.9
1937	106.9	43.1	102.6	14.3	78.7
1938	108.4	41.6	106.6	19.0	81.4
1939	107.9	42.1	109.1	17.2	81.6
1940	107.5	42.5	110.7	14.6	83.6
1941	106.7	43.3	114.9	9.9	81.2
1942	105.7	44.3	118.9	4.8	77.5
1946	106.7	43.3	138.1	4.2	85.1
1947	107.6	42.4	134.8	3.9	87.3
1948	108.3	41.7	136.4	3.8	96.6
1949	109.0	41.0	142.8	5.9	100.0
1950	108.9	41.1	155.8	5.3	98.4
1951	108.3	41.7	151.3	3.3	95.9
1952	108.0	42.0	156.2	3.1	92.9
1953	108.5	41.5	163.6	2.9	93.4
1954	109.6	40.4	169.4	5.6	92.2
1955	108.4	41.6	176.6	4.4	92.0
1956	108.1	41.9	184.3	4.2	92.0
1957	108.8	41.2	188.1	4.3	92.4
1958	109.1	40.9	189.0	6.8	93.5
1959	109.2	40.8	195.2	5.5	94.2
1960	109.0	41.0	200.0	5.6	95.0
1961	108.8	41.2	202.0	6.7	96.0

Source: U: See text. Other series: See Table 5-B.

lationship may actually be found by using a value of e which would yield an absurd result for one or two years (i.e., in which P(L) was negative). To explore this possibility, price of leisure series were computed for e equal to 5.0, 6.0, 7.0, and 8.0. Finally, as a check on our assumptions, absurd values of e, e=−1 and e=−2, were selected to see if they would yield perverse regression results.

These various price of leisure series were then used to compute series of nominal income (wH+LP(L)) and of the expanded price index (α+βP(L)). From these series, forty-six series of real income and relative prices were obtained. (Thus $Y' = \dfrac{LP(L)+wH}{\alpha+\beta P(L)}$ and $P(L)' = \dfrac{P(L)}{\alpha+\beta\, P(L)}$ where $P(L) = W(1\text{-Ue})$.)

f. Estimating Equations for Leisure Time Demand Model

The following equations were fitted by the least squares method.

A. Full employment years model
   1900-1961 (10 observations)
   A.1. $L = a + bW$
   A.2. $L = a + bW + cP(R)$
   A.3. $L = a + bw' + cP(R)'$
   A.4. $H = gW_0{}^r\, P(R)^s$

Five variants of $W_0{}^{14}$ were computed: A-4-1, $x = 0$; A-4-2, $x = 2$, $z = 40$; A-4-3, $x = 2$, $z = 35$; A-4-4, $x = 3$, $z = 40$; and Λ-4-5, $x = 3$, $z = 35$.

B. Annual Variations Model
   1929-1961 (30 observations)
   B.1. $L = a + bW$
   B.2. $L = a + bW + cP(R)$
   B.3. $L = a + bW' + cP(R)'$
   B.4. $L = a + bP(L)' + cP(R)' + dY'$

In B.4., forty-six values of e were selected from 0.1 to 4.0 by tenths, and $e = -2.0$, -1.0, 5.0, 6.0, 7.0 and 8.0. For each of these forty-six values, Y' and $P(L)'$ were calculated for each of thirty observations, and a multiple regression was then run.

14. See pp. 103-5 above for a discussion of these empirical fatigue functions.

TABLE 5-E

Leisure time demand model: statistical estimates from
full employment model, 1900-1961 (10 years)

Estimating equations*	Coefficient of determination (adjusted)	Simple coefficient of correlation of w, P(R)	Test statistic: autocorrela- tion of residuals†
A.1L = 89.79 + .116W (.017) [.108]	.831	—	.64
A.2L = 107.80 + .095W − .158P(R) (.018) (.081) [.089] [− .159]	.875	−.588	1.48
A.3L = 85.99 + .182W′ − .042P(R)′ (.060) (.026) [.206] [− .060]	.964	−.956	1.80

* Figures in parentheses are estimates of the standard errors of the regression coefficients. Figures in brackets are elasticities calculated at the observed means of the variables.   .
† Test statistic is the Durbin-Watson d.

g. *Regression and Correlation Results for Leisure Time Demand Model*

Leisure time is regressed against the real wage rate in a simple correlation in A-1. A-2 introduces estimates of the relative price of recreation as a second explanatory variable. In A-3, estimates of the wage rate and the price of recreation are deflated by a correction factor (of the form $a + \beta W$). This has the effect of extending the consumer price index to include leisure.[15]

The coefficients of multiple correlation, adjusted for degrees of freedom, are high, and rise in each successive formulation (see Table 5-E).

The partial regression of wage on leisure time appears to be significant in all three regressions. The regression coefficient of the price of recreation is more significant in the conventional multiple regression than in the regression using deflated variables. The significance of both independent variables was reduced by dividing them by a common price index. This deflation increased the level of the simple coefficient

15. See pp. 101-3 above.

of correlation between wages and the price of recreation from .59 to .96.

Autocorrelation among the residuals is reduced from a significant to an insignificant level when the price of recreation is added as an explanatory variable. These results give support to the following hypotheses:

1. That there has been a backward bending supply curve of hours worked per employee in the United States, 1900 to 1961, for wage and salary workers in the private, non-agricultural sector; that is, that the income effects of wage increases have outweighed the substitution effects, so that one observes a positive relation between the wage rate and the demand for leisure time. This relationship continues to be observed when the price of recreation is held constant.

2. That there is a negative relationship between the relative price of recreation and the demand for leisure time.

One should be careful in comparing the relative sizes of these elasticity estimates. For example, a comparison of these measures in Equation 2 shows that the elasticity of demand for leisure time with respect to the price of recreation is estimated to be almost twice that of the elasticity with respect to the real wage rate. But this does not mean that changes in the relative price of recreation were twice as important as changes in the wage rate in bringing about a decline in the work week.

From 1901 to 1961 the relative price of recreation dropped by about one-fifth. The real wage rate quadrupled in the same period. Hence, somewhat less than one-fourth of the calculated decline [16] in hours is due to changes in the price of recreation, more than three-fourths to changes in the wage rate.

h. Statistical Results Using Fatigue Models

The statistical results obtained from fitting equations A-4-1 to A-4-5 are given in Table 5-F.

When fatigue is present, average hourly earnings will rise more rapidly than the base wage. When the fatigue effect is suppressed, they will rise at the same rate. Substituting a base wage for average hourly earnings would tend to produce a wage series which rises more rapidly in recent years. But the time series of hours and wage rates presented

16. The calculated decline exceeded the actual drop by 1.8 hours.

in Table 5-C would lead one to expect that the apparent response of hours to changes in the conventionally measured wage rate has in the last thirty years been reduced, not increased. Hence, one would expect that the substitution of a base wage for average hourly earnings would reduce the correlation between hours of work and the wage rate.

A reduction of the correlation coefficient is observed (Table 5-F) as the fatigue effect is introduced, although this reduction is quite minor. A somewhat more important result is the increase in the absolute values of the regression elasticities.

The exponents of w and of P(R) should be read, respectively, as $r = \frac{b+c}{1+xc}$ and $s = \frac{d}{1+xc}$. For example, in A-4-5, $r = \frac{b+c}{1+3C}$, while in A-4-1, $r = b + c$. Therefore, the increase in $/b+c/$ or in $/r/$ as we go from A-4-1 to A-4-5 would be considerably greater than that implied by the increases in r or s.[17]

A third hypothesis in the leisure time demand model that gains support from these regressions is that the neglect of the fatigue factor both understates the elasticity of hours with respect to the wage rate and tends to obscure the role of other factors, such as the price of recreation, in the determination of the work week.

17. These five regressions were also run without P(R) as an explanatory variable. The regression and correlation results were quite similar to those in Table 5-F. However, autocorrelation among the residuals was much higher. The Durbin-Watson d ranged from 1.14 to 1.22.

TABLE 5-F

*Leisure time demand model: statistical estimates from full employment model
with the assumption of output-reducing fatigue, 1900-1961 (10 years)*

Estimating equations*			Adjusted coefficient of determination	Test statistic: autocorrelation of residuals†
A-4-1 x = 0 H = 105.9W	−.236 (.024) P(R)	.118 (.115)	.955	1.62
A-4-2 x = 2, z = 40 H = 95.9W	−.249 (.028) P(R)	.146 (.125)	.946	1.61
A-4-3 x = 2, z = 35 H = 101.2W	−.257 (.030) P(R)	.150 (.128)	.942	1.62
A-4-4 x = 3, z = 40 H = 92.6W	−.254 (.030) P(R)	.157 (.128)	.942	1.60
A-4-5 x = 3, z = 35 H = 100.0W	−.266 (.033) P(R)	.160 (.133)	.938	1.63

*† See notes to Table 5-E.

i. Correlation Results of Leisure Time Demand Model (Annual Variations Model)

Table 5-G gives regression and correlation results for Equations B-1 to B-5. The coefficient of determination rises from equation one [18] to equation two, from equation two to equation three, and from equation three to equation four. Those improvements show that the use of, respectively, the price of recreation, a more appropriate price index, and unemployment each contribute to a better estimate of the data.

However, the regressions in the annual models in B-4 yield similar correlation coefficients. This gives practically no guidance at all in the selection of e, the measure of the responsiveness of the price of leisure to unemployment.

Moreover, in the regression analysis below, conclusions as to the signs of the three regression coefficients and their significance are also independent of the choice of e. However, variations in the point estimates of the coefficient are large, particularly in the case of the income and price of leisure coefficients.

Intercorrelation among the three independent variables is high for all forty values of e. A common effect of intercorrelation is that regression coefficients will not be significant, even though the coefficient of determination is significant and close to 1. In the present model, significance, as measured by the 't' ratios of the regression coefficients, is not markedly affected by our choice of e.

Some insight into the versimilitude of these several estimates of e can be obtained indirectly by an analysis of the plausibility of the leisure demand elasticities that they yield.

Estimates of the income elasticity of demand for non-working time, holding the price of this time constant, were made by Jacob Mincer, in his *Labor Force Participation of Married Women*. Mincer's results show an income elasticity of .33,[19] approximately the same result obtained in this study when e is assumed to be equal to four.

---

18. The much lower R^2's in equations B-1 to B-3 than in equations A-2 to A-3 are probably due to the restriction on the A model to years of relatively full employment.
19. He obtains an income elasticity of work with respect to income of —.83. This may be translated as an elasticity of leisure with respect to income of +.33 if hours of leisure are defined as in this study. It should be pointed out though that Mincer's income variable is somewhat different than ours, since it is designed to represent permanent rather than current income.

TABLE 5-G

Leisure time demand model: statistical estimates from annual variations model using first differences of the time series, 1929-1961 (excluding 1943-1945)

Estimating equations*	Coefficient of determination (adjusted)	Test statistic: autocorrelation of residuals†
B-1 $L = 103.16 + .032W$ $(.007)$ $[.041]$	.405	.48
B-2 $L = 110.25 + .041W - .093P(R)$ $(.008) \quad (.048)$ $[.052] \quad [-.077]$	.461	.59
B-3 $L = 116.43 - .003W' - .093P(R)'$ $(.050) \quad (.037)$ $[-.004] \quad [-.080]$	.556	.67
B-4-a $(e = 0.1)$ $L = 89.65 + 3.645Y' - 532.62P(LY) - 3.19P(R)'$ $(.758) \quad (110.68) \quad (3.06)$ $[6.814] \quad [-6.620] \quad [-.028]$	.738	.67

TABLE 5-G (continued)

Estimating equations*				Coefficient of determination (adjusted)	Test statistic: autocorrelation of residuals
B-4-b (e = 1.0)	$L = 91.70$	$+ .448Y'$ (.076) [.895]	$54.25P(L)'$ (9.26) [.653]	$- 3.55P(R)'$ (2.92) [-.033]	.726	.67
B-4-c (e = 2.0)	$L = 93.32$	$+ .271Y'$ (.039) [.500]	$- 28.73P(L)'$ (4.852) [-.330]	$- 3.78P(R)'$ (2.70) [-.038]	.720	.67
B-4-d (e = 3.0)	$L = 95.05$	$+ .209Y'$ (.027) [.381]	$- 20.47P(L)'$ (3.85) [-.221]	$- 4.03P(R)'$ (2.44) [-.045]	.713	.68
B-4-e (e = 4.0)	$L = 96.88$	$+ .175Y'$ (.022) [.314]	$- 16.52P(L)'$ (3.34) [-.161]	$- 4.29P(R)'$ (2.13) [-.054]	.705	.69
B-4-U (e = 5.0)	98.80	$+ .152Y'$ (.018) [.264]	$- 14.27P(L)'$ (2.84) [-.114]	$- 4.53P(R)'$ (1.74) [-.068]	.696	.70

115

TABLE 5-G (continued)

Estimating equations*				Coefficient of determination (adjusted)	Test statistic: autocorrelation of residuals†
B-4-V (e = 6.0) 100.76	+.132Y' (.016) [.208]	− 12.68P(L)' (2.21) [−.049]	− 4.67P(R)' (1.25) [−.101]	.680	.71
B-4-W (e = 7.0) 101.60	+.109Y' (.015) [297]	− 10.15P(L)' (1.45) [− 3.663]	− 3.97P(R)' (.66) [−.099]	.637	.54
B-4-X (e = 8.0) 106.66	.037Y' (.011) [.097]	− 4.04P(L)' (2.19) [−.113]	− 1.95P(R)' (1.42) [−.024]	.196	.58
B-4-Y (e = − 1.0) 88.74	−.233Y (.079)	+ 49.71P(L)' (15.61)	− 3.14P(R)' (3.28)	.739	.67
B-4-Z (e = − 2.0) 87.38	−.057Y' (.047)	+ 24.10P(L)' (10.54)	− 2.96P(R)' (3.43)	.745	.67

*† See notes to Table 5-E.

Table 5-E showed various estimates of the elasticity of leisure time with respect to the price of recreation from the full employment model. Of these, equation A-3 is most comparable to the B-4 group of Table 5-F. The price of recreation elasticity of the full employment model of 6 percent is most closely approximated by an e equal to 4.

Finally, an income elasticity of 1.5 [20] or more is unlikely, since it would imply that the addition of property income would yield such an increase in leisure time taken that there would be a *decline* in money income. Since this is not a common experience one would be suspicious of those results (e.g., those arising from e equal to 0.1) that would only be consistent with such unorthodox behavior.

Thus, estimates based on the middle or upper values of e would be preferred to those based on lower values.

j. Regression Results for Leisure Time Supply Model (Annual Variations Model)

The statistical results summarized in Table 5-G show that the hypothesis of the 'backward bending supply curve of hours' is supported by the results of equations B-1 and B-2. A positive regression between leisure time and the wage rate is observed in equation B-3, but the 't' value of the regression coefficient is almost zero. The drop in the value of the 't' ratio from equation B-2 to equation B-3 is presumably due to the rise in the coefficient of determination between our measures of the wage rate and of the price of recreation.

The most interesting feature of a regression analysis of equation(s) B-4 is probably the separate estimates of the effect of income and of the price of leisure on leisure time that it affords. These elasticities are observed to be positive and negative respectively, with fairly high observed values of the 't' ratios.

The income elasticity of leisure is larger than the price of leisure elasticity for all values of e, thus offering further support to the backward bending supply curve theory.[21]

The regression of leisure time on the price of recreation is negative throughout. This is consistent with the notion of complementarity between recreation and leisure time.

Equations B-4-Y and B-4-Z show that absurd values of e do indeed

20. See Mathematical Note 5A in the Appendix.
21. See OWEN, 'The Supply of Labor', p. 327, for a mathematical analysis of this point.

yield perverse results. The analysis of equations B-4-U–X is somewhat more complicated. Only equation B-4-X, which says that the price of leisure is negative when the unemployment rate exceeds 12.5 percent, yields obviously inferior results. Equations B-4-U and B-4-V show marginally lower coefficients of determination, and have somewhat higher 't' values for the regression coefficients. However, it would appear that violating the condition that $P(L) \geq 0$ for several observations does not change the regression or correlation results very much.

The regressions based on the equations B-4-a–e are characterized by a significant degree of autocorrelation in the residuals. Since such auto-correlation tends to produce underestimates of the standard errors of the regression coefficients (as well as overestimates of the coefficient of determination) it tends to weaken the regression analysis.

Equation B-4-c was run in the form of first differences. The results are shown in Table 5-H. In this form, the test statistic indicates non-significant autocorrelation. The regression coefficients and the estimates of their standard errors are somewhat larger than in the original results, but do not indicate any important change in the earlier regression analysis.

TABLE 5-H

Leisure time demand model: statistical estimates from annual variations model using first differences of the time series 1929-1961 (excluding 1943-1945)

Estimating equations*	Coefficient of determination (adjusted)	Test statistic: autocorrela-tion of residuals†
$L = -.037 + .292 \Delta Y' - 31.46 \Delta P(L)' - 4.54 \Delta P(R)'$ (.098) (8.74) (3.65)	.340	1.94

*† See notes to Table 5-E.

k. Possible Biases in Income and Price of Leisure Variables

The wage rate data used in this study may be biased downwards since 1940. These wage rates are based on the non-agricultural employee group, including women and students. The hours data used are esti-

118

mated net of women and students since 1940.[22] Since employed women and teenagers characteristically receive lower hourly wages than do adult males,[23] and since the proportion of women and students in the employee group has been rising since 1940,[24] their inclusion would tend to pull down the estimate of wages.[25]

Another possible bias is created in the income estimates due to the omission of property income accruing to employees. The share of property in total income has been measured as declining over time (at least in the 1929 to 1945 period).[26] If this economy-wide pattern held true for the employee group, then the measure used here has overstated the rate of increase that took place in employee income.

These two biases may offset each other in a comparison of two endpoints (e.g., 1900 to 1961 or 1929 to 1961). Even so, it is not that the less extensive comparisons would be free of bias. The decline in reported property income was completed by the closing years of World War II. The effects of including women and students only bias the wage data after 1940.

In any case, only the first bias would affect the price of leisure variable, biasing it downward over time. Thus the absolute size of the price of leisure elasticity may be overestimated here.

Other possible sources of bias in the income and price of leisure variables elasticities may be found in the problem of measurement raised in the discussion of education, commuting, and government finance. It was concluded tentatively there that the rise in the educational level of the work force and the possible increase in daily commuting time [27] would tend to retard the increase in leisure time, while

22. Before 1940, *movements* in hours included those of women and students, though the *level* was linked (in 1940) to estimates made net of women and students. See above, Chapter 3.

23. LONG, *The Labor Force*, pp. 355-56.

24. See Chapter 3, above.

25. A probable offset to this bias may be found in the decline over time in these wage differentials. See LONG, *The Labor Force*, pp. 355-56.

26. Irving KRAVIS, 'Relative Income Shares in Fact and Theory', in Irwin Friend and Robert Jones, editors, *Proceedings of the Conference on Consumption and Saving, A Study of Consumer Expenditures, Incomes and Savings* (Philadelphia: University of Pennsylvania, 1960), II, 391-99.

27. The addition of the relative price of transportation had little or no effect on the regression results. The 't' value of the price of transportation variable was close to zero. See OWEN, 'The Supply of Labor', pp. 309-18.

the secular increase in government activity may have accelerated it. It would of course be difficult to pinpoint the net effect of these biases.

l. An Alternative Model of the Demand for Leisure Time

The regression of leisure on income in the annual variations models in equations B-4 a-3 might be biased by the inclusion of the dependent variable, leisure time (L), in the measure of income (Y), since the measure of income, Y, used there includes the dependent variable, leisure time, L. (Current value of income $= wH + P(L)L = w(K-LUe)$.) Since there is a negative short-run relation between L and Y here, and since we obtain a positive net regression of L on Y, the effect of the bias probably is to underestimate this regression coefficient.

In order to correct this, a variant on equation B-4 may be used in which leisure time is not on the right side of the equation.

If E is the employment rate ($E = 1 - u$), income and the price of leisure might be written as $Y = wE^{k_1}$ and $P(L) = wE^{k_2}$.

From the analysis in section 2.11, 'Unemployment and Hours of Work', one would expect k_1 and k_2 to be greater than zero and k_2 to be greater than k_1.

Then the demand for leisure time, L, could be estimated in the exponential form:

$$(1) \quad L = aY^{B_1}P(L)^{B_2}P(R)^{B_3}$$

Using $Y = wE^{k_1}$ and $P(L) = wE^{k_2}$, equation (1) can be rewritten as:

$$(2) \quad L = a(wE^{k_1})^{B_1}(wE^{k_2})^{B_2}P(R)^{B_3} \text{ or:}$$

$$(3) \quad L = aw^{B_1 + B_2}E^{k_1B_1 + k_2B_2}P(R)^{B_3}$$

Letting $B_1 + B_2 = B_4$ and $k_1B_1 + k_2B_2 = B_4$, the last equation is a simple exponential relationship in L, w, E, and P(R):

$$(4) \quad L = aw^{B_4}E^{B_5}P(R)^{B_3}.$$

This equation was estimated to thirty years in the 1929 to 1961 period. The results are shown in Table 5-I.

The positive sign of the estimate of B_4 shown there supports the hypothesis that $B_1 + B_2$ is greater than zero. This result is consistent with the earlier finding of a backward bending supply curve of hours of work in this period, in equations B-4 (see Table 5-G).

The negative sign of the observed value of B_5 in Table 5-I means that $k_1B_1 + k_2B_2$ is estimated to be less than zero.

120

If (as one would expect) k_1, k_2, and B_1 are all greater than zero, and B_2 is less than zero, then the positive sign of B_4, taken in conjunction with the negative sign of B_5, might indicate that k_2 is greater than k_1, that is, that the price of leisure shows a greater relative reaction to changes in employment than does real income.[28]

TABLE 5-I

Leisure time demand model: statistical estimates from exponential annual variations model, 1929-1961 (excluding 1943-1945)

Estimating equations*			Coefficient of determination (adjusted)	Test statistic: autocorrelation of residuals†
.075	−.146	−.033		
(.009)	(.032)	(.030)		
L = 210.9W	E	P(R)	.712	.58

*† See notes to Table 5-E.

m. Conclusions

The following major conclusions gain support from the regression analyses:

1. There is a positive relation between income and the demand for leisure and a negative relation between the price of leisure and the demand for leisure.

2. The income effect of a rise in the real wage rate is greater than the substitution effect. Thus, when income and price-of-leisure elasticities are estimated separately, the former is greater than the latter in each of the forty estimates. Moreover, the elasticity of leisure time with respect to the wage rate is positive.

3. There is an inverse relation between the relative price of recreation and the demand for leisure time. These results would be consistent with the hypothesis that leisure time and recreation are complements, rather than substitutes, in consumption.

28. Two other variants of equation B-4 were also employed. In one the weighting of money income and leisure in the income variable was altered in order to give a smaller weight to leisure. In the other, the depressed nineteen thirties were omitted. In both cases, the results were rather similar to those in Table 5-G.

4. The introduction of fatigue models increased the values of both the wage rate and price-of-recreation elasticities.

The correlation analysis showed that the conventional estimates of the demand for leisure time can be improved by introducing the price of recreation as an explanatory variable, by introducing leisure into the estimate of income and the estimate of the consumer price index used in the demand analysis, and by introducing the assumption that the price of leisure falls relative to the wage rate as unemployment rises.

The supply of labor by the individual to the firm has been estimated thus far in a single-equation regression model. Regressions based upon these single-equation methods will tend to yield estimates of the standard errors of the regression coefficients which are biased downwards. Estimates of the regression coefficients will also be distorted, although the direction of the bias may be more difficult to determine.

An alternative and in some ways superior approach would be to estimate the supply of labor function as part of a system of equations which would include as a member the equation for firm demand for hours of work per worker.

In the next section a statistical model of firm demand for labor is developed and tested. These supply and demand analyses are combined in section 5.3, where, using the two-stage least squares technique, new measures of some of the labor supply parameters estimated in the present chapter are obtained.

5.2 THE EMPLOYER DEMAND FOR HOURS OF WORK

In order, then, to obtain better estimates of the demand for leisure time, a two-equation model, which would include the employee demand for leisure time equation and an employer demand for hours of work relationship, should be developed, and estimated simultaneously.

The Construction of an Employer Demand for Hours of Work Model

The first step in building this two-equation model will be to construct a model for employer demand for hours of work. An underlying assumption of the employer demand for hours of work relation is that

122

changes in the average hours of work of employees in the economy will change the wage rate.

The basic argument for this view is that increases in the supply of labor will, ceteris paribus, reduce labor's marginal product and, hence, the hourly wage rate. This argument is quite consistent with the assumption, made in the employee demand for leisure time model, that individual employers would be indifferent (within conventional limits) as to the hours schedules set in their plants.[29]

Such variations in the hours schedules of individual firms will not have a significant influence on the supply of labor or on wage rates in the economy as a whole. However, if all the employees and workers of the United States (or a significantly large proportion of them) do decide to work longer hours (perhaps because of a rise in the relative price of commercial recreation) then, at the same level of labor force participation, there will be an increase in the overall supply of labor. This shift may have the effect of depressing the level of hourly wages.

Thus, it is not inconsistent to argue that while there exist employers who, in the long run at least, are indifferent to the level of hours of work per worker, a shift by employees in general to preferences towards longer hours of work will depress the general wage level.

An empirical test of the possible inverse relationship between hours of work and the hourly wage rate may be made with the help of a simple time series model. Let the hourly real wage that employers are willing to pay in full employment conditions be a function of the capital-labor ratio (C), the quality of labor supplied (Q), and a factor (T) that represents the residual of economic growth that cannot be explained by increases in factor inputs. (T would thus be a function of technical change, and other factors.[30])

Thus, letting K = capital stock, N = labor employment (approximately equal to labor force at full employment), and H = hours worked per employee, the capital-labor ratio, C, may be written:

$$(1) \quad C = \frac{K}{NHQ},$$

29. Exceptions to this are examined in section 5.1 and again in the present section in those models where output per worker is allowed to rise non-proportionately to hours of work (see equations A-4-2 – A-4-5 in Table 5-F and equations 2–5 in Table 5-J).
30. See Edward F. DENISON, *The Sources of Economic Growth in the United States* (N.Y.: Committee for Economic Development, 1962) for a description of these other factors.

and the demand for labor equation might be written:

(2) $\dfrac{W}{Q} = F(C,T),$

where $\dfrac{W}{Q}$ is the efficiency wage of labor.

If the elasticity of the real hourly wage rate with respect to the capital-labor ratio is constant (as is true when the real wage rate equals the marginal product of labor and the production function is of the Cobb-Douglas type, and shows constant returns to scale), then the demand for labor equation (d) might be rewritten:

(3) $\dfrac{W}{Q} = aC^bT.$

Letting $F = \dfrac{K}{NQ}$ and $S = TQ$, (3) may be written for the purposes of statistical estimation as:

(4) $W = aF^bH^{-b}S.$

A variant of this model was employed to incorporate the effects of fatigue on effective labor supply, and hence, on the wage rate. The fatigue model employed in the supply equations (where $P(L) = W_0 \left(\dfrac{Z}{H}\right)^x$ if $H \geq Z$ and $P(L) = W_0$ if $H \leq Z$) was employed here to obtain estimates of W_0 for several values of Z and X (see above, pp. 103-5, for the method used).

Using this fatigue model one may then write:

(5) $W_0 = aF^b[F(H)]^{-b}S.$

MH^n yielded a very good approximation to $F(H)$ for several values of x and z within the relevant range of hours variation, and it was used in this model:

(6) $W_0 = am^{-b}F^bH^{-bn}S.$

Description of the Data for the Demand Model

The wages and hours of work data used to estimate this demand model were obtained from the supply model developed in section 5.1. The remaining data needed for this model – employment,[31] quality of labor, capital stock,[32] and residual growth[33] – were obtained for the years 1909-

---

31. E.F. DENISON, *Sources of Economic Growth in the United States*, p. 37, col. 1.
32. *Ibid.*, p. 141, col. 5.
33. Adjusted to eliminate agriculture.

1913 to 1957 from E. F. Denison's *Sources of Economic Growth in the United States.*

Denison uses a quality of labor variable that is adjusted for changes in the age-sex composition of the labor force, for the level of education, and, rather arbitrarily, for the operation of fatigue. Since the model used in this study makes its own (arbitrary) adjustments for fatigue, Denison's education and labor force composition variables [34] were used to form a modified quality variable (Q).

Denison's data were exteended from 1909 to 1901 by methods that were similar to those he used for the post-1909 period.

Following Denison, Kendrick's *Productivity Trends in the United States* [35] was used for employment data and the 1940 *U.S. Census of Population* for education.[36] The same residual growth trend was used for 1901 to 1909 as for later years. Capital stock estimates were made a little differently than Denison's.[37] Goldsmith's estimates of reproducible, tangible capital in constant prices (net of government-owned capital, the monetary stock, and consumer durables) were used.[38] The resulting capital stock series was then linked to Denison's series in 1909.

Biases in the Data for the Employer Demand Model

In these models, movements in the wages and hours series of non-farm employees are explained in terms of measures of capital stock, labor force, education, and residual growth for the civilian economy as a whole.

These explanatory variables should explain the general wage level. Changes in the general wage level in turn should explain in the long run much, but not all, of the movement in the wages of non-farm employees. In addition to shorter run dynamic differences, long-run divergence would be produced by changes in these factors (both equalizing and

34. P. 85, cols. 2 and 3, respectively.
35. Table A-VI.
36. Kendrick gives his labor force composition adjustment for 1900. This was used with a linear interpolation to obtain estimates for 1901 and 1906.
37. But carrying the series forward to 1915, almost identical results for the 1909-1915 period were obtained.
38. Raymond GOLDSMITH, *A Study of Savings in the U.S.* (Princeton: Princeton University Press, 1956).

non-equalizing) that account for the differential in wages in equilibrium between the total labor force and the average group of non-farm employees.[39]

A possible source of measurement error may also be found in Denison's residual growth trend estimate. Denison believes that the fatigue factor is so strong that, in the 1909 to 1929 period, the reduction in hours per man had no negative effect on total output. The hours estimates in the present study would indicate an effective labor loss of from about 5 percent (if $x = 3$ and $z = 35$) to about one-sixth (if no fatigue effect exists). Since labor is but one factor of production, production losses of a somewhat smaller nature would be implied. Nevertheless, if the fatigue effect was not as strong as the rather drastic effect Denison envisages, the residual growth trend is an underestimate in the earlier years.

Employer Demand Analysis: Regression and Correlation Results

The employer demand for labor equation, $w = am^{-b}F^bH^{-bn}S$, was fitted to a time series of sixteen years of relatively full employment, the ten full employment years used in the supply analysis (see pp. 99-100) plus those years in the post-1929 period [40] in which the unemployment rate was less than 4.5 percent. The sample was enlarged so that these results could be utilized in conjunction with the two-equation model results described in the next section.[41]

39. Differential changes in wage rates might also be reflected in differential changes in the capital-labor ratio; i.e., as the relative price of labor in this sector rose, capital might be substituted for labor here (and labor for capital elsewhere). But differential changes in the capital-labor ratio might also occur as a result of a non-neutral technical change in the production function in the industry or sector. Such a change need have no long-run effects on relative sector wages.

Of course, changes of this sort in the economy-wide production function that is being used here would also implicitly contradict our model.

40. Annual data were not available before 1929 for some series needed for the two-equation model.

41. As a check on the validity of this extension, equations 1 and 4 were run with the original ten peak years. As a check on the accuracy of our extension of the Denison data back to 1901, the pre-1913 years were eliminated from the sample, and equations 1 and 4 regressed with the resulting subsample of fourteen years. In each of these cases, the regression and correlation results were similar to those shown in Table 5-I. None of the conclusions in the text would have to be changed if one of the alternative samples were used.

TABLE 5-J

Employer demand for hours of work model: statistical estimates from full employment model, 1900-1961 (16 years)

Estimating equations*				Unadjusted R^2	Test statistic: autocorrelation of residuals†
		F	S		
1	x = 0: W = .037H	−.668 (.312)	.325 (.118)	1.390 (.131)	.997	2.10
2	x = ½, z = 40: W = .017H	−.549 (.306)	.311 (.115)	1.406 (.128)	.997	2.11
3	x = 1, z = 40: W = .008H	−.421 (.308)	.297 (.116)	1.427 (.129)	.997	2.12
4	x = 2, z = 40: W = .001H	−.235 (.299)	.287 (.112)	1.451 (.125)	.997	2.12
5	x = 3, z = 35: W = .116H	024 (.302)	.287 (.113)	1.443 (.126)	.996	2.04

*† See notes to Table 5-E.

The resulting regression and correlation estimates are shown in Table 5-J. The correlation coefficients are all very high.

The regression coefficient of the wage rate on the capital-labor ratio F is near 0.3 in all four results. A comparison of this result with equations 3 and 4 on page 124 shows that an estimate of the exponent of F of 0.3 is consistent with a Cobb-Douglas production function with an elasticity of output with respect to capital of .3 and to labor of .7.

The variable H, hours per employee, is a proxy variable for F(H), labor input (approximated by $F(H) = mH^n$). In the fatigueless case, $n = 1$, implying that output per individual employee rises in proportion to hours per employee. In the other equations, n ranges downward to about three-quarters for $z = 40$, $x = 2$ and to about one-half for the stronger fatigue case $z = 35$, $x = 3$. Since one would expect the coefficient of mH^n to have the same absolute value as that of F, one would expect a coefficient of H of about −.3 in equation 1, −.2 to −.25 for equations 3 and 4, and −.15 for equation 5. On this basis, equation 4, with the fatigue assumptions $z = 40$, $x = 2$, would appear to be preferable. In this equation −bn is estimated at −.235 (the coefficient of H). This is quite close to the value that one would predict from the estimate of b (.29, the coefficient of F) and the calculated value of n (about three-quarters).

It is noteworthy that the regression results (though not the correlation results) in these demand equations are much more sensitive to the choice of a fatigue model than were the demand for leisure time equations (cf. Table 5-F and also Table 5-K). In the demand equations, when one sets $z = 35$ and $x = 3$, the regression of w on H is virtually eliminated.

The regression coefficient of H in the preferred equation 4, while negative as expected, is not statistically significant. Therefore, one could not reject, on the basis of these results, the hypothesis that the wage rate offered by employers is insensitive to hours of work per employee.

The regression coefficients of S, the technology-quality variable, are greater than their expected value of unity. This might be due to a number of factors, including the problems of relating wage movements in one sector of the economy to demand and quality conditions in the whole, and of correctly estimating the residual growth trend.

So far, the employer demand for labor and the employee demand for leisure time have been estimated separately, in single-equation models. In this section, they are estimated simultaneously, thus correcting the bias in the regression coefficients in the two sets of single-equation estimates.

Let us first write the equations in a similar form:[42]

(1) $w = A_1 + B_1H + C_1P(R) + u_1$ Supply of Labor
(2) $w = A_2 + B_2H + C_2F + D_2S + u_2$ Demand for Labor

In this formulation, w and H are endogenous variables, and $P(R)$, F and S are exogenous variables.

Equations (1) and (2) can be solved for H as:

$$(3)\ H = \frac{A_2 - A_1 + C_2F + D_2S - C_1P(R) + u_2 - u_1}{B_1 - B_2}$$

Substituting this value of H in equation 1 we see that if $B_1 - B_2 < 0$,[43] then $r(H, u_1) > 0$, and $r(H, u_2) < 0$. It can be shown[44] that these correlations will tend to yield biased estimates of regression coefficients when they are obtained by a least squares, single-equation method.

In general, the standard errors of the coefficients will be underestimated. The biases produced in the estimates of the coefficients are more complicated. It can be shown that for a large enough sample one would expect the following results (capital letters represent true values; lower case letters, single-equation, least squares estimates; the designation of regression coefficients continues to follow that in equations (1) and (2) above:

$$B_1 < b_1 \text{ and } B_2 > b_2$$

Moreover, further inferences about the biases in the single-equation parameters may be deduced from our knowledge of the observed data.[45] For example:

42. In Table 5-K, a logarithmic rather than a linear model was employed. As the model is linear in the logarithms of the variables, this difference would not affect the statement about biases in this section.
43. As one might expect from the single-equation estimates of these parameters. See, for example, the single-equation estimates in Table 5-K.
44. See Mathematical Note 5B in the Appendix.
45. See Mathematical Note 5B in the Appendix.

$$/B_1/ > /b_1/ \quad \text{(since } b_1 < 0)$$
$$/B_2/ < /b_2/ \quad \text{(probable, since } b_2 < 0)$$
$$c_1 < C_1 \quad \text{(since } r(P(R),H) > 0)$$
$$C_2 > c_2 \quad \text{(since } r(H,F.S) < 0)$$
$$D_2 > d_2 \quad \text{since } r(H,S.F) < 0)$$

In order to correct such biases, the two-stage, least squares method was employed to estimate equations 1, 2 and 3. [The two-stage, least squares method first obtains estimates of H from the reduced form (equation 3), and then, substituting these estimates of H for actual H in equations 1 and 2, carries out classical least squares regressions.] The resulting estimates are shown in Table 5-K. Single-equation estimates are also given, in order to see the biases introduced by this form of estimation.[46]

In a large sample, the two-equation estimates of the regression parameter would be likely to be free of the single-equation biases analyzed above. For such a sample, one could take the regression coefficients obtained in two-equation estimates, substitute them as 'true value' estimates in the inequalities above, and hope that the inequalities would hold.

Considering that the results of Table 5-K are based on a quite small sample, it is noteworthy that one may still substitute these regression coefficients into the inequalities above and obtain the expected results in *every* case.

In the employee supply of labor (demand for leisure time) analysis the estimate of the regression coefficient of wage rate on hours and its standard error are little affected by the introduction of a second equation. However, the regression coefficient of wage rate on price of recreation is increased considerably, thus bringing into clearer focus the relationship between the demand for leisure time and the price of recreation observed earlier. This relationship is also seen in the reduced form estimates of the table. In both the single-equation and the two-equation estimates, the employer supply of labor estimates are little affected by the choice of fatigue model.

The most striking change produced in the demand analysis by the introduction of a second equation is the reduction of the absolute value of the estimated elasticity of wage rate with respect to hours. In the single-equation demand analysis the fatigue model with $x = 2$, $z = 40$

---

46. These single-equation estimates of the supply of hours will differ somewhat from those presented in section 5.1 as they are based on a sample of 16 years.

TABLE 5-K

Employer demand and employee supply of hours of work

Regression analysis estimates of elasticities
(Figures in parentheses are estimates of standard errors of elasticities)*

Dependent variable: W

| | Demand | | | | Von Neumann |
	H	F	S	R²	statistic
x = 0					
Single	−.668	.325	1.391	.996	2.10
Equation	(.312)	(.118)	(.132)		
Two Stage	−.570	.333	1.430	.995	2.12
Least Squares	(.784)	(.134)	(.367)		
x = ½, z = 40					
Single	−.549	.311	1.407	.996	2.11
Equation	(.307)	(.115)	(.128)		
Two Stage	−.378	.326	1.478	.995	2.13
Least Squares	(.770)	(.131)	(.346)		
x = 1, z = 40					
Single	−.418	.298	1.429	.996	2.13
Equation	(.309)	(.116)	(.129)		
Two Stage	−.181	.318	1.525	.995	2.14
Least Squares	(.817)	(.140)	(.334)		
x = 2, z = 40					
Single	−.234	.287	1.451	.996	2.13
Equation	(.299)	(.112)	(.125)		
Two Stage	.044	.311	1.565	.995	2.14
Least Squares	(.757)	(.129)	(.310)		
x = 3, z = 35					
Single	.029	.288	1.440	.995	2.12
Equation	(.302)	(.113)	(.126)		
Two Stage	.255	.307	1.540	.995	2.14
Least Squares	(.744)	(.127)	(.304)		

* All equations fitted to logarithmic form.

TABLE 5-K

	Supply			Von Neumann statistic
	H	P(R)	R^2	
x = 0				
Single	−4.086	.270	.959	.85
Equation	(.305)	(.384)		
Two Stage	−4.403	.570	.994	1.08
Least Squares	(.121)	(.149)		
x = ½, z = 40				
Single	−4.020	.289	.957	.86
Equation	(.307)	(.387)		
Two Stage	−4.343	.594	.995	1.09
Least Squares	(.113)	(.140)		
x = 1, z = 40				
Single	−3.956	.307	.944	.86
Equation	(.311)	(.392)		
Two Stage	−4.281	.615	.995	1.09
Least Squares	(.109)	(.134)		
x = 2, z = 40				
Single	−3.838	.321	.951	.85
Equation	(.315)	(.397)		
Two Stage	−4.169	.635	.995	1.09
Least Squares	(.124)	(.124)		
x = 3, z = 35				
Single	−3.551	.310	.942	.86
Equation	(.314)	(.396)		
Two Stage	−3.880	−.622	.995	1.10
Least Squares	(.099)	(.122)		

TABLE 5-K

	F	P	S	R²
		Reduced Form		
		Dependent Variable: W		
x = 0	.383	−.085	1.643	.996
x = ½, z = 40	.357	−.057	1.617	.996
x = 1, z = 40	.328	.028	1.592	.996
x = 2, z = 40	.308	.006	1.549	.996
x = 3, z = 35	.292	.004	1.442	.996
		Dependent Variable: H		
	−.058	.153	−.370	.963

TABLE 5-L

Empirical estimates of time series used in demand and supply of hours of work model, full employment model, 1900-1961 (16 years)

	H	W $x=0$	W_0 $x=\frac{1}{2}$ $z=40$	W_0 $x=2$ $z=40$	W_0 $x=3$ $z=35$	P(R)	F	S
1901	58.4	45.0	46.4	49.9	56.8	121.9	.817	.729
1906	57.0	50.5	51.8	55.4	62.7	121.0	.822	.770
1913	55.0	54.6	55.8	59.0	66.2	92.5	.850	.831
1919	50.0	67.0	67.7	69.8	76.2	97.6	.872	.883
1923	49.6	77.0	77.8	80.0	87.2	103.8	.933	.927
1926	49.3	78.0	78.8	80.9	88.0	96.4	.974	.962
1929	48.7	83.2	84.0	85.9	93.2	96.9	1.000	1.000
1946	43.3	138.1	138.3	138.6	145.7	85.1	.762	1.370
1947	42.4	134.8	134.9	135.2	140.9	87.3	.781	1.397
1948	41.7	136.4	136.9	136.5	141.6	96.6	.788	1.426
1951	41.7	151.3	151.4	151.6	157.1	95.9	.800	1.514
1952	42.0	156.2	156.3	156.5	162.7	92.9	.804	1.544
1953	41.5	163.6	163.6	163.8	169.5	93.4	.805	1.575
1955	41.6	176.6	176.7	176.8	183.2	92.0	.845	1.635
1956	41.9	184.3	184.5	184.7	191.8	92.0	.846	1.665
1957	41.2	188.1	188.1	188.2	194.3	92.4	.866	1.694

yields the most reasonable results, while in the two-equation analysis, it yields perverse results. Using the two-equation technique, the fatigue model with $x = 1/2$, $z = 40$ yields elasticities of the expected sign, but the absolute value of the hours elasticity is rather higher than one would expect.[47] Most probably, regression coefficients of the expected sign and magnitude could be generated by selecting a fatigue model intermediate between these two ($z = 40$, $1/2 < x < 2$). One would conclude then that models that use a relatively mild fatigue effect ($x = 40$, $z = 1/2$ or 2) yield better results than those in which greater fatigue is assumed.

5.4 THE DEMAND FOR MARKET RECREATION AND THE DEMAND FOR LEISURE TIME

The complementary relationship between leisure time and commercial recreation which was observed in the analyses of the employee demand for leisure time in sections 5.1 and 5.3 is explored in this section in the context of the demand for commercial recreation. More specifically, data on changes in the price and quantity of leisure time are used in an attempt to improve upon a conventional analysis of the demand for market recreation. The complementarity hypothesis is further explored by observing whether changes in the price of leisure are, ceteris paribus, inversely related to the demand for recreation.

The time series data presented in Chapter 4 appear to show that commercial recreation has been a superior good in the United States. Thus, one would expect that a conventional analysis of the demand for recreation would show that it has a positive income elasticity as well as a negative own price elasticity.

Moreover, from the empirical analysis of leisure time in sections 5.1-5.3, which showed that the demand for leisure time had an inverse relationship to the price of recreation, one would expect that the demand for recreation would be reduced by increases in the price of leisure.

The conventional analysis of the demand for market recreation suppresses the price of leisure as an explanatory variable. It can be shown that this neglect of the price of leisure will probably give a downward bias to estimates of the income elasticity of market recreation. Income and the price of leisure are highly intercorrelated (see section 5.1

47. See p. 128 above.

134

above). Hence, a rise in income will usually be accompanied by a rise in the price of leisure. If the demand for a consumer good which is 'independent' of leisure (i.e., has a weak subsitute relationship with leisure) is being estimated, then a rise in the price of leisure will probably have a slight positive effect on the demand for this consumer good. If the consumer good is a close substitute for leisure, this positive effect will be much greater. But for a consumer good that is complementary with leisure, the reasoning is reversed, and one expects a reduction in the observed income elasticity. Hence, the suppression of the price of leisure variable underestimates the income elasticity; an unbiased method should yield higher estimates of the income elasticity of market recreation.

Estimation of the Demand for Market Recreation in a Conventional Model

The demand for market recreation was regressed on conventional measure of income and on the relative price of recreation. Data for recreation demand were obtained from Table 4-C, data for the relative price of recreation from Table 4-B, column 2. Income is measured by real disposable income per capita.

Data for the years 1929 to 1961 (omitting the war years 1943 to 1945) were utilized. A least squares fit to linear models produced the results in equation 1 of Table 5-M. These results indicate that recreation is a normal good with an income elasticity approximately equal to unity and a quite small price elasticity.

The conventional model was first modified by introducing L, or leisure time per employee, as an explanatory variable. This method of introducing leisure into the analysis would be the most acceptable if one assumes that leisure time is determined outside the market system, so that the worker-consumer is confronted with weekly income, weekly work hours, and the price of recreation.

Statistical results derived from the conventional estimation of market recreation with leisure time as an independent variable are given in equation 2 of Table 5-M. They show that the introduction of leisure into the model in this way has little effect on the income or price elasticity of demand, or on the coefficient of correlation. The coefficient of leisure time in the second regression equation is approximately equal to zero.

The low value of the observed leisure time regression coefficient may be due in part to the fact that a measure of the leisure time of one sector of the population, wage and salary workers in the private, nonagricultural sector, is being used in conjunction with market demand data for the population at large. This divergence may not be too important in measuring long-term movements, but is likely to be troublesome in a series using annual data, and hence may account in part for the poor results here. This problem is discussed at greater length on pp. 138-40 below.

TABLE 5-M

Market recreation model: statistical results derived from conventional model, annual variations, 1929-1961, excluding 1943-1945

Estimating equations*	Adjusted coefficient of determination
1. $R = 15.6 + .586Y_c - .196P(R)$ $(.024)$ $(.110)$ $[1.028]$ $[-.266]$	.963
2. $R = 17.8 + .587Y_c - .197P(R) - .020L$ $(.029)$ $(.113)$ $(.375)$ $[1.030]$ $[-.267]$ $[.033]$	.962

* See notes to Table 5-E.

The Use of Employee Models in Estimating the Demand for Market Recreation

The models used in the next two sections attempt to incorporate the relationship with leisure time in a somewhat more sophisticated fashion. The models are modified versions of those employed in estimating the demand for leisure time in section 5.1 above. They differ from the conventional demand model in that money income and hours of work are both determined within the system (rather than being treated as exogenous variables).

Again, two sets of years were examined: ten years of low unemployment in the 1900 to 1961 period, selected to analyze the determination of demand under conditions of approximately full employment, and thirty years in the 1929 to 1961 period, selected to measure demand under more typical conditions of both full and less than full employment. Recreation demand data were obtained from Table 4-C;

136

recreation price data from Table 4-B, column 2, and from the indexes used to derive equation B-4-c.

Estimation of the Demand for Market Recreation in the Full Employment Employee Model

The demand for market recreation is estimated here in the full employment employee model developed in section 5.1. This model uses ten years, characterized by full employment and spaced at least three years apart. The full employment model has an advantage in estimating the demand for market recreation in that movements in the wage rate of wage and salary groups are likely to be a better indicator of those in the population in a full employment model than they would be in a model that analyzed year-to-year fluctuations.[48] This model has a serious empirical disadvantage in estimating complementarity between leisure and recreation in that income and the price of leisure are here assumed to be perfectly correlated. Hence, it is not possible to obtain the net regression of recreation on the price of leisure.

Yet it might be possible to explore such complementarity between leisure and recreation as does exist from another angle. Only part of the changes in leisure time that take place are explained by changes in income, the price of leisure, and the price of recreation. Other factors such as unionization, legal regulation, changes in taste, and changes in consumer technology may also help to determine the demand for leisure. If complementarity exists, these 'unexplained' changes in leisure might be expected to have a positive effect on the demand for market recreation.

In any event, the leisure time demand regressions in section 5.1, 'The Demand for Leisure Time', showed that, in full employment at least, these other factors appeared to play a quite minor role in the determination of the demand for leisure. The residuals are quite small and thus probably had but a small effect on recreation sales.

Residual errors from the full employment leisure time model (Table 5-E, equation 2) were calculated and were added as a third explanatory variable in the full employment recreation demand model. A least squares fit to the ten observations using these variables yielded the results shown in Table 5-N, where 'z' is the residual error in the leisure time estimate.

48. See pp. 56-57 above.

137

The demand equation for recreation estimated here appears to be normal with a positive income and a negative price elasticity. The observed income elasticity is almost unity. If, as one would predict, the elasticity of demand for market recreation with respect to the price of leisure is negative, this observed income elasticity is an underestimate.

Finally, the sign of the residual leisure variable is positive, and thus is consistent with the notion of complementarity. However, it is not statistically significant. This is not surprising, since most of the variation in leisure time had been explained in the full employment model. The residuals were quite small, indicating that factors other than income, the price of leisure, and the price of recreation played a minor role in the determination of the demand for leisure time. In the next section, the price of leisure itself is used as a determinant of the demand for market recreation.

TABLE 5-N

Market recreation model: statistical results derived from full employment employee model: 1900-1961

$(n = 10)$

Estimating equation*	Adjusted coefficient of determination	Autocorrelation test statistic†
$R = 34.43 + .424W - .289P(R) + .0003Z$ $\quad\quad\quad (.037) \quad\quad (.163) \quad\quad\quad (.0008)$ $\quad\quad\quad [.885] \quad [-.650] \quad\quad\quad\quad **$	.964	1.42

*† See notes to Table 5-E. ‹

** $Z = 0$ at its mean.

Estimation of the Demand for Market Recreation in the Annual Variations Employee Model

This model follows the annual variations model used in the estimation of the demand for leisure time in section 5.1. Thirty years in the 1929-1961 period are employed. However, it is necessary here to use some-

138

what different measures of the independent variables, income and the price of leisure. The income and the price of leisure of employed wage and salary workers vary cyclically as a result of fluctuations in the number of hours worked per worker. But these fluctuations do not reflect the fact that the number of employees shrinks (and the number of unemployed rises) during a depression. The neglect of this second aspect of cyclical fluctuation was possible when the demand for leisure time per employed worker was being estimated. Fluctuations in employment cannot be neglected in the analysis of the demand for a good sold to the entire population – market recreation.

A crude attempt was made here to fill this gap by giving the unemployed an income and price of leisure of zero and obtaining a simple weighted average of the two groups for each variable.

Demand-for-recreation data were then regressed against a linear combination of the income, price of leisure, and relative price of recreation data,[49] and a least squares fit was obtained. The results, using e = 2.0, are shown in Table 5-O.

TABLE 5-O

Market recreation: statistical results derived from modified employee model, annual variations, 1929-1961

(n = 30, e = 2.0)

Estimating equation*			Adjusted coefficient of determination	Autocorrelation test statistic†
$R = -11.41$ $+ 1.246Y''$ (.572) [3.12]	$- .946P(L)''$ (.539) [−1.49]	$- .285P(R)'$ (.129) [−.36]	.930	1.37

*† See notes to Table 5-E.

These results are consistent with the theories that market recreation is a normal good, with a positive income and a negative price elasticity, and that it has a negative cross-elasticity of demand with leisure time.

49. Income and price of leisure are after-tax estimates.

Moreover, the size of the parameters indicates that it has a high income elasticity, and is quite responsive to changes in the price of leisure time.

The 't' ratios of the regression coefficients are generally high, and the coefficients of determination are both quite high.

This employee model relies upon certain assumptions about the income and price of leisure of economic groups not measured here (i.e., that they are related to the income and price of leisure of employees and of the unemployed). It is also possible to develop synthetic measures of income and the price of leisure which are themselves plausible (if somewhat controversial) estimates, but which will yield nonsense results when applied to the analysis of recreation demand.[50] These measures partly reflect the necessary subjectivity in the various modifications in income and price estimates.

However, they also reflect the problems that arise from the aggregate recreation industry data themselves. Thus, when one takes the simpler recreation component, reading (as measured by the sale of newspapers, magazines and books), and analyzes the demand for reading, by means of the various synthetic estimates, reasonable results are obtained in each case.[51] The depression in aggregate recreation sales in the nineteen thirties was led by the decline in sales of radio sets, yet the number of sets in use (see pp. 87-89) actually increased.[52] This important role played by the large stock of relatively new radio sets in existence in 1930 will tend to bias the results obtained from estimating a model that works with current sales by the recreation industry in the nineteen thirties.

Conclusions

These results would suggest the following conclusions:

50. This was done in OWEN, 'The Supply of Labor', pp. 340-42.
51. *Ibid.*, pp. 344-46. In the modified employee model, income and price of leisure elasticities of about unity were obtained for reading. However, reading demand has not shown the same long-term response to increases in income as has total market recreation (cf. the discussion of reading in Chapter 4). The higher short-run income elasticity of the demand for market recreation is probably due in part to its durable component and in part to a higher long-run income elasticity. One might guess, then, that the long-term elasticity of market recreation would lie between unity and the value given in Table 5-O.
52. It will be recalled that *increases* in stocks of durable goods in use was not characteristic of the thirties.

(1) Recreation is a normal, superior good in that it has a positive income elasticity and a negative own-price elasticity. Price elasticity is fairly low (one-half or less), indicating an inelastic demand. Income elasticity (when the price of leisure is held constant) is quite high.

(2) It was argued in Chapter 2 that leisure and recreation were 'complementary' in the sense that they are used together in consumption. In the present chapter, tests are offered of the hypothesis that the two goods are complementary in the sense that they have negative cross elasticity of demand. The market recreation data and regressions presented in this chapter shed some light on this subject and, in general, do tend to support the view that leisure and recreation are complementary in this more strict sense.

5.5 THE DEMAND FOR LEISURE ACTIVITY

The preceding work has supported the hypothesis that leisure time and recreation are complements in consumption. In the present section, a modification of the Becker leisure activity model [53] is employed which assumes that leisure time and recreation are actually inputs into leisure activities.

A comparison of the results obtained by using this model with the regression results obtained by estimating the demand for leisure and recreation separately may yield some further understanding of the relationship between leisure and recreation.

The Empirical Model

In this section the demand for leisure activity of male wage and salary employees in the private, non-agricultural sector is estimated for thirty years in the 1929 to 1961 period, and for ten full employment peak years, 1901 to 1961.

The quantity demanded of leisure activity (A) was measured as a weighted average of the inputs leisure time (L*) and market recreation (R).

53. See section 2.3 for a discussion of the leisure activity model. The model used in the empirical work here differs from Becker's in several ways. In this measure of the cost of time no distinction is made between more and less valuable time. Moreover, fixed weights for leisure time and market recreation are used, while Becker would probably prefer changing weights.

Leisure time estimates were derived from measures of consumption or leisure time estimates of the employee group as shown in section 5.1. Leisure time is defined in the present analysis as that time spent in recreational activities. It is thus a much more restricted notion of leisure than the consumption time measure of leisure (L) used in section 5.1, which included all time spent in consumption activities. The measure used in the present section excludes time used in sleeping, eating and the like. For the empirical work of the present section, leisure time (L*) is measured as all consumption time over ten and one-half hours a day. The estimate of the amount of time spent at leisure in the more restricted sense was adopted upon examination of the time budgets presented in Table 4-A. It is, of course, a rather rough estimate of the base level of leisure time. More important for the time series analysis, it involves the implicit assumption that all changes in consumption time since 1929 have been changes in leisure time.

An index of demand for market recreation per capita (see Table 4-C) was used to estimate changes in recreation demand by wage and salary workers.

An examination of hours of leisure, average hourly compensation of wage and salary workers, and average expenditures on market recreation in the 1947-1949 period led to the conclusion that a maximum of 10 percent of leisure activity input was market recreation (i.e., a minimum of 90 percent was time). Moreover, this maximum can only be accepted by ignoring the value of time of non-employee members of the family. A potential source of bias operating in the opposite direction is of course the neglect of important forms of market recreation by the Department of Commerce estimates.

This measure of leisure time and the index of market recreation demand were then linked in a nine to one proportion in estimates for the year 1948 to obtain a rough measure of the level of leisure activity, A, in that year. Using these fixed weights, estimates were carried back to 1901, and forward to 1961.

A model of the form $A = F(Y, P(A))$, where Y is real income per worker and P(A) is the relative price of recreation activity, was used to analyze the demand for leisure activity in the years 1929 to 1961.

In the annual variations model real income per worker Y′ was taken from section 5.1 (see Table 5-G, equation B-4-C). An e value of 2.0 was chosen for the analysis in this model. P(A)′, the relative price of leisure activity, was estimated by a weighted average of the relative

142

price of recreation (P(R)′) and the relative price of leisure (P(L)′). The two input prices were derived from Chapter 5.1.[54] The weighting procedure was the same as that used in the estimation of A.

This method yields (see Mathematical Note 5C in the Appendix) an index of the relative price of leisure activities of the form:

$$\frac{P(A)_1}{P(A)_0} = .9\frac{P(L)_1}{P(L)_0} + .1\frac{P(R)}{P(R)_0}$$

In the 1901 to 1961 full employment analysis, the real hourly wage rate (see Table 5-B, column 5) was used as a proxy for real income. P′(A) was a weighted average of W′ and P(R)′ (again using a nine to one proportion).

Changes in Consumer Technology and Measurement Errors in the Leisure Activity Model

It was necessary to use an index of 'factor inputs', i.e., leisure time and recreation, to measure the more abstract leisure activities, since there is no market in the activities themselves. Insofar as the consumer technology of leisure activity has been improved by the consumer's more efficient use both of his leisure time and of his recreation goods (rather than by quality improvements in the leisure time and recreation goods themselves) his factor index would underestimate the growth in leisure activity.[55] If this indeed be the case, there is an upward bias over time in these estimates of the relative cost of leisure activities, as well as a downward bias in leisure activity.

Empirical Results

The statistical results in Table 5-P are consistent with the theory that leisure time and market recreation may be considered together as a consumer good, with a positive income and a negative price elasticity. They are also consistent with the theory that a reasonable approximation to the relative price of this activity is obtained by the market price of its inputs.

The last equation (equation 4), relates the demand for leisure activ-

---

54. Again at e = 2.0. These prices are also taken from equation B-4-C of Table 5-G.
55. However, it should be pointed out that the same reasoning yields similar critiques of disposable income and of non-leisure time as well.

ity to the price of recreation and of leisure time separately. As might be expected from the relative weights of leisure time and market recreation in the composition of leisure activity, the elasticity of this activity with respect to the relative price of leisure time is much greater than is its elasticity with respect to the relative price of market recreation.

TABLE 5-P

Leisure activity model

Estimating equations*	Adjusted coefficient of determination	Autocorrelation test statistic†
Full Employment Model (10 Years, 1901-1961)		
A = 8.485 + .502W′ − .259P′(A)	.982	1.85
(.092) (.138)		
[1.883] [−1.164]		
Annual Variations Model (30 Years, 1929-1961)		
A = 16.79 +.296Y′ −.268P′(A)	.857	.75
(.031) (.041)		
[1.532] [−.973]		
A = 19.54 +.291Y′ −.273P(L)′ −.048P(R)′	.835	.76
(.035) (.044) (.024)		
[1.506] [−.880] [−.135]		

*† See notes to Table 5-E.

5.6 THE ELASTICITY OF SUBSTITUTION BETWEEN LEISURE TIME AND MARKET RECREATION

The two regression equations in Table 5-Q show the results of an attempt to estimate the elasticity of substitution between leisure time and market recreation in leisure .activity.[56] This elasticity of substitution, x, was estimated in the annual variations model in the form: $R/L = a(P(R)/P(L))^x$.[57] In the full employment peaks model, $w = P(L)$ and the form

56. The symbols employed in Table 5-Q correspond to those in Table 5-P, explained in the text, pp. 141-43.
57. This form makes the implicit assumption that leisure activity is a linear homogeneous function of its inputs.

144

$R/L = a(P(R)/w)^x$ is employed. The results in Table 5-Q suggest that the absolute value of the elasticity of substitution, x, is somewhat greater than one-half.[58] This estimate then tends to reject the hypothesis that leisure time and market recreation are used in fixed proportions (in which case x would be equal to zero).

However, the elasticity of substitution, x, does appear to be relatively small. A small elasticity of substitution between leisure time and market recreation in leisure activity would, in conjunction with the larger price elasticity of demand for leisure activity observed in section 5.5, suggest that a complementary relationship exists between leisure time and market recreation. This point is developed more systematically in the following section.

TABLE 5-Q

Statistical estimates of the elasticity of substitution between leisure time and market recreation

Estimating equations*	Adjusted coefficient of determination	Autocorrelation test statistic†
Full Employment Model (10 Years, 1901-1961)		
−.512		
(.064)		
(1) R/L* = .10(P(R)′/w′)	.875	1.82
Annual Variations Model (30 Years, 1929-1961)		
−.607		
(.036)		
(2) R/L* = .10(P(R)′//P(L)′)	.907	.76

*† See notes to Table 5-E.

58. When using the annual variations data, autocorrelation was significant in the statistical estimation of both the leisure activity and elasticity of substitution models. These equations were therefore estimated in the form of first differences. Here, autocorrelation was reduced to insignificant levels in both cases. In first differences, the price elasticity of demand for leisure activity was estimated at −1.17 and the elasticity of substitution between leisure time and market recreation at −.78.

145

5.7 A COMPARISON OF SOME EMPIRICAL RESULTS OF THE LEISURE ACTIVITY, LEISURE TIME, AND MARKET RECREATION ANALYSES

The demands for leisure time and market recreation have now been estimated separately (sections 5.1 and 5.4) and, jointly, in the leisure activity (section 5.5) and elasticity of substitution (section 5.6) models. A comparison of the four sets of results may offer a further test of the relationship between leisure and recreation.

Annual Variations Models, 1929-1961

Table 5-R below presents regression results, in the form of elasticities computed at the mean values of the variables, for leisure time, market recreation, leisure activity, and the goods-time mix in leisure activity. These elasticities are all derived from the annual variations model (thirty years, 1929 to 1961) with e = 2.0 (measuring the price of leisure $P(L) = W(1-2.0U)$, where U is the unemployment rate).[59] The market recreation estimates are from the modified employee model.[60] Mean values for leisure time used in computing the elasticities in equation 1 are based upon the restrictive notion of leisure time (L*) developed in section 5.5 (i.e., leisure time as recreation time, rather than consumption time). These models are not strictly comparable, of course, since the leisure time demand series refers to employees, and the market recreation series to the population as a whole.

If these models were exact, one would expect the following results (see Mathematical Note 5D in the Appendix for a mathematical analysis):

Let: L* = Quantity Demanded of Leisure Time
  R = Quantity Demanded of Market Recreation
  A = Quantity Demanded of Leisure Activity
  P(L) = Price of Leisure Time
  P(R) = Price of Market Recreation
  P(A) = Price of Leisure Activity
  $\bar{L}$* = Expenditure on Leisure Time = L*P(L)
  $\bar{R}$ = Expenditure on Market Recreation = RP(R)
  $\bar{A}$ = Expenditure on Leisure Activity = AP(A)
  AP(A) = LP(L) + RP(R)
  E_{yz} = Elasticity of y with respect to a change in z
  x = Elasticity of substitution between R and L.

59. See pp. 106-8 above.
60. See pp. 138-40 above.

Then: (1) $E_{R,P'(L)} = \dfrac{\bar{L}}{\bar{A}} (E_{A,P'(A)} - x)$

(2) $E_{L,P'(R)} = \dfrac{\bar{R}}{\bar{A}} (E_{A,P'(A)} - x)$.

Thus leisure time and market recreation will be complements (in the sense that a decline in the relative price of leisure – holding real income and the relative price of recreation constant – will increase the demand for market recreation, and vice versa) if the price elasticity of demand for leisure activity is larger than the elasticity of substitution between leisure time and market recreation (cf. the discussion of this point in section 2.3 above). Table 5-R presents evidence that the price elasticity of demand for leisure activity does exceed the elasticity of substitution between leisure time and market recreation. Taken together with the negative signs of the price of recreation coefficient in the leisure time demand equation and the price of leisure coefficient in the market recreation demand equation, this statistical evidence offers further support to the hypothesis that leisure time and market recreation are complements in this annual variations model.

With an exact model, one would also expect the following relations to hold:

(3) $E_{R,P'(R)} = \dfrac{\bar{R}}{\bar{A}} E_{A,P'(A)} + \dfrac{\bar{L}}{\bar{A}} x$

(4) $E_{L,P'(L)} = \dfrac{\bar{L}}{\bar{A}} E_{A,P'(A)} + \dfrac{\bar{R}}{\bar{A}} x$.

Comparing (2) and (3), one would predict that, if there is some substitution between leisure time and market recreation in leisure activity, the recreation price elasticity in the recreation demand equation would be larger than that in the leisure demand equation. Similarly, comparing (1) and (4), one would expect the leisure time price elasticity in the leisure time demand equation to be larger than that in the recreation demand equation. The data in Table 5-R support the first but not the second expectation. However, both of these results may simply reflect the rather high income and price of leisure time elasticities of demand for market recreation obtained in the annual variations model. Higher elasticities for sales of market recreation than for the demand for leisure time may be found in an annual variations model if cyclical variation in market recreation sales (especially of durable appliances) exaggerates the fluctuations in recreation services consumed.[61]

61. See pp. 138-40 above.

TABLE 5-R

Selected empirical results of employee models, annual variations model (e = 2.0), 1929-1961, excluding 1943-1945

Source in Chapter 5	Form of equation	Dependent variable	Elasticity at mean with respect to			
			Y′	P(L)′ P(R)′ P(A)′		P(R)′/P(L)′
Leisure time Table 5-G Equation B-4-c	Linear	L*	1.56	−1.03 −.12		
Market recreation Table 5-O	Linear	R	3.12	−1.49 −.36		
Leisure activity Table 5-P Equation P-4	Linear	A	1.53	−.97		
Elasticity of substitution Table 5-Q Equation 2	Logarithmic	$\overline{\dfrac{R}{L}}$				−.61

Complementarity and Substitution, 1900-1961: The Full Employment Years Model

The full employment model (ten years, 1900-1961) covers a much longer period of time than does the annual variations model (30 years, 1929-1961). The longer period saw a much wider range of values of the several variables of the series, and provides some interesting material for the study of complementarity and substitution in determining changes in the demand for leisure and recreation.

The income and price of leisure are perfectly correlated in this model. Hence it is not feasible to regress R on P(L). However, when L was regressed on P(R) in the full employment peaks model (see the text table opposite), a negative relation was found, thus supporting the hypothesis of complementarity between leisure time and market recreation.

Moreover, a comparison of the price elasticity of demand for leisure activity found in the full employment peaks model with the elasticity of substitution between market recreation and leisure time in those years

148

(see the text table below) shows a larger value for the price of leisure activity elasticity. As in the annual variations model, these results further support the hypothesis that market recreation and leisure time are complements.

Full employment models (10 years, 1900 to 1961)[62]

	Wage rate elasticity	Price of recreation elasticity
Leisure time	0.32	− 0.58
Market recreation	0.89	− 0.65

	Price of leisure activity elasticity	Elasticity of substitution
Leisure activity '	− 1.16	− 0.51

The estimate of the elasticity of substitution in the text table suggests that leisure time and market recreation are not used in fixed proportions. Some additional evidence of substitution between leisure time and market recreation (i.e., of the two being used in variable proportions in leisure activity) may also be seen in this text table. The price of recreation elasticity is larger in the demand for recreation equation than in the demand for leisure time equation. Moreover, the wage rate elasticity in the demand for leisure time regression is larger than that in the demand for recreation equation. These results would both suggest that a substitution in favor of market recreation in leisure activity would have taken place as the relative price of recreation declined and the relative price of leisure time increased.

Some further insight into the relationship between leisure time and market recreation in these years may be gained by an inspection of Table 5-S, which shows some of the relevant data for this period. Column 1 gives estimates of leisure time, L^* (consumption time over ten and one-half hours a day). An index of consumption of market recreation, R^* (equal here to one-ninth of leisure time in 1948), is presented in column 2. Column 3 gives the ratio of the price of recreation (ratio equal to 100 in 1948) to the price of leisure (equal here to the wage rate). Column 4 shows the ratio of recreation to the quantity demanded

62. Leisure time estimates are derived from equation A-2, Table 5-E. Market recreation estimates are from Table 5-N.

149

of leisure time and column 5 shows the ratio of the current value of recreation to the current value of leisure time.

TABLE 5-S

Long-term relationships between the demand for leisure time and the demand for market recreation

	Quantity demanded				Expenditure on R
	Leisure	Market recreation	$\dfrac{R*}{L*}$	$\dfrac{P(R)}{W}$	$\dfrac{\bar{L}}{\bar{R}}$ (Expenditure on L)
	L*	R*			
1901	18.1	1.1	.057	3.82	.217
1906	19.5	1.3	.063	3.38	.215
1913	26.5	1.8	.066	2.06	.136
1919	26.5	1.8	.066	2.06	.136
1923	26.9	1.9	.070	1.90	.133
1926	27.2	2.3	.082	1.75	.143
1929	27.8	2.9	.104	1.64	.171
1948	35.2	3.9	.111	1.00	.111
1953	35.5	4.4	.124	.81	.100
1956	35.2	4.9	.140	.70	.099

See text for adjustment of data for this table.

These data show that while both leisure time and market recreation have risen over the past half century, the ratio of market recreation to leisure time rose from one seventeenth to one seventh. The ratio of the price of recreation to that of leisure fell from 3.8 to .7. This was, presumably, an important reason for the shift in the proportion in which the two goods were consumed.

Finally the data in column 5 of Table 5-S indicate that in current dollars the share of leisure, or foregone earnings, in leisure activity has risen, and that of market recreation has declined. Using these calculations, an observer in 1900 would have concluded that leisure time represented about four-fifths of the total cost of leisure activity, while in 1956 an observer would say that over nine-tenths of leisure activity costs incurred were attributable to leisure time.

However, when account is taken of price changes the data show that substitution actually took place in the opposite direction. The fact that the ratio between expenditures moved in favor of leisure time in the face of a rising price for leisure may attest to the relative inelasticity of substitution between the two goods.

150

5.8 SOME GENERAL EMPIRICAL CONCLUSIONS AND SUGGESTIONS FOR FURTHER RESEARCH

The Demand for Leisure Time

Perhaps the most interesting question posed by the empirical work of this chapter is whether the innovations suggested in Chapter 2 for measuring the effects of the price of leisure and the price of recreation shed any light on the income-leisure choice under modern conditions. If they do seem useful, what improvements might be made in their utilization? Which innovations from Chapter 2 not tested in the present chapter might prove to be useful in subsequent empirical investigations of the work-leisure choice? Let us first examine the role of each of the innovations in the analysis of demand for leisure time that were introduced in the empirical study.

The Wage Rate. The simple regression of the demand for leisure time on the real wage rate yielded the expected positive relationship. Thus, support was given to the hypothesis that there is a backward-bending supply curve of labor. Somewhat more powerful support is given to this hypothesis when a positive partial relation between leisure time and the wage rate is observed when the relationship is obtained in multiple regressions which include the relative price of recreation and the employment rate. And still further support is given when the positive relationship continues to hold when estimated in a two-equation system, which includes an employer demand for hours of work relation.

The Price of Recreation. In the full employment model of leisure time, the introduction of the price of recreation as an explanatory variable in the demand for leisure time significantly reduced the level of autocorrelation among the residuals. The leveling off of the relative price of recreation since 1929 offers a partial explanation of the observed retardation in the rate of decline over time in hours of work.

Introduction of Leisure Time into Measures of Income and the Price Index generally led to important improvements in the correlation analysis.

Unemployment Rate. The introduction of the employment (unemployment) rate permitted the price of leisure to move countercyclically and thus generally improved the correlation analysis. Moreover, it made it possible to obtain estimates of income and the price of leisure as functions of the wage rate and the unemployment rate which had the important property that they were not perfectly intercorrelated. Thus

151

it was then possible to obtain separate estimates of the price and of the income elasticities of leisure time. These estimates in turn offered further support to the backward bending supply curve of labor hypothesis.

Fatigue. The introduction of fatigue into the measure of the price of leisure led to higher calculated values of the regression coefficients, and a somewhat lower correlation coefficient. This suggests that the omission of fatigue leads to underestimates of the income and price estimates of the demand for leisure time and to overestimates of the coefficient of determination.

The Demand for Market Recreation

The empirical estimation of the demand for market recreation as a function of real income, the relative price of recreation, and the relative price of leisure showed that it was a superior good with a negative own-price elasticity.

The use of the price of leisure as a regressor permitted a better measurement of the income elasticity of the demand for recreation. The income elasticity observed here was much higher than that observed in the conventional analysis (which suppresses the price of leisure).

The Demand for Leisure Activity

The demand for leisure activity analysis yielded positive income and negative price elasticities; it was thus consistent with economic theory, and with the expectations formed from the earlier regressions. Similarly, the direct observation of the elasticity of substitution between leisure time and market recreation yielded a small, negative relationship, thus offering (in conjunction with the income elasticity of leisure activity) further support to the complementarity hypothesis.

Suggestions for Further Research on the Income-Leisure Choice

These results, then, seem to be interesting enough to encourage further work. There are two roads which an investigator might take. The first approach would lead to the more thorough analysis of the variables that have been included in this study. An important task here would be to improve upon the raw data employed. Equally important would

152

be improvements in the way in which these variables are utilized in the various estimating equations.[63]

New data could also be collected which would supplement existing series. For example, the analysis of leisure activities could be extended if time budgets were available which gave not only the time input of activities, but also the goods input. If such information were collected periodically, on a sample basis, then some very interesting results indeed could be expected. In particular, the estimation of the expansion parameter and of the elasticity of substitution for individual recreation activities could yield quite interesting results.[64]

The second road would involve the use of additional explanatory variables in the modern work-leisure choice.

An analysis of improvements in working conditions over time and of the relationship of these improvements to the leveling off of the work week in recent decades might be quite fruitful. One might start by asking whether the relative cost of providing good working conditions has declined in some relevant sense since, say, the nineteen thirties. Information on these costs might be quite difficult to obtain directly. However, indirect measures (for example, the growth of white collar occupations, the decline of coal mining and other changes in the occupational mix) might yield some interesting results.

Again, it was shown in Chapter 2 that the proliferation of commuting[65] and of educational opportunities would raise the price of leisure and hence tend to slow down the reduction in the work week. If this proliferation has been stepped up in recent decades, it may account in part for the relatively slow growth in leisure time in recent decades.

Another very important factor in determining the work week, but one which might be rather difficult to quantify, is the prevailing system of incentives. If an entrepreneur, for example, feels that an extra hour

63. For example, both the fatigue and unemployment functions are assumed to be constant over time. Yet with changes in the occupational mix and in management practices one would expect that both the way in which output varied with hours of work and the reluctance of employers to lay off their employees would change over time.

64. Some interesting empirical work has been done by the U.S. Government on the analysis of dollar expenditure per hour of recreation time spent at public outdoor recreational facilities. See, for example, *National Recreation Survey*, O.R.R.R., Study Report No. 19 (Washington, D.C.; Government Printing Office, 1962).

65. At least, if commuting time is included in the work week.

of work per day on his part will make the difference between bankruptcy and financial success (even in spite of the fatigue effect), he will ordinarily put in that extra hour. Similarly, a white collar worker who believes that extra hours will lead to promotion may well do the same. Some control of the incentive factor is provided in this study by the exclusion of entrepreneurs and of agricultural workers from the data. However, it is quite possible and even probable that important shifts in the incentive function took place within the non-farm employee group in the past sixty years.[66]

The Development of a System of Simultaneous Equations for the Leisure-Recreation Markets

The estimation of hours of work in a demand, then in a two-equation model provided some rather interesting results, which generally concorded with received economic theory. However, the supply of labor equation estimated in the two-equation system differed little from that in the single-equation model. Thus, one can conclude that the omission of the second equation did not seriously bias the earlier results.

Further work might be done by expanding the system to include the relevant market recreation equations. Since the markets for recreation and leisure time are interconnected, it might be argued that further work should be done by expanding the system to include supply and demand equations for market recreation. The demand for market recreation equation could be taken from one of those used in this study, along with the employer demand for labor and employee supply of labor functions. To complete the system, a supply of recreation equation might be developed: $R_s = f_{4(w,P(R),V)}$, where V is a vector of the relevant costs of providing recreation goods and services. One could then write (at least for the full employment years analysis):

(1) $H_s = f_1 (w,P(R))$ (4) $R_s = f_4 (w,P(R),V)$
(2) $H_d = f_2 (w,F,S)$ (5) $H_s = H_d$
(3) $R_d = f_3 (w,P(R))$ (6) $R_s = R_d$

66. Some factors that might have contributed to such shifts would be: the growth of the large corporation, the development of management science, the growth of the white collar sector, the smaller percentage of ambitious young men who start their own businesses (all positive), the rise of the trade union movement, the development of class consciousness, and the curtailment of immigration from abroad and from farms into American industry (the last four negative).

154

where equations (1) and (2) are derived from the two equation model for hours of work presented in Table 5-N, and equation (3) is similar to the market recreation analysis shown in Table 5-N.

In this system, H, R, w and P(R) are endogenous variables, and F, S, and V are exogenous. If one can write the first four equations in a linear form (or one that is linead in the logarithms) then one can solve for each of the exogenous variables in terms of the three exogenous variables, and then obtain the reduced form coefficients.

These calculations were not carried out in the present study, because of the anticipated difficulty in obtaining time series estimates of the recreation cost variable V. This would have involved obtaining time series estimates of cost functions in each of a number of commercial recreation industries.

If P(R) is not affected by R, the omission of the supply equation should not bias the demand equation estimates. The very profusion of recreation industries might stand us in good stead here, if such rising cost industries that exist are offset by declining cost industries.

However, it is possible that the demand for recreation estimates are biased,[67] since the observed technical improvements in many of the recreation industries may have had a common cause: i.e., a rapid growth in consumer demand. In any event, it would be of some interest to see estimates of V, the costs of recreation, and what effect their introduction into the analysis would have on this system of equations.

67. But with R^2 close to unity in the demand for market recreation analysis, it is unlikely that this bias would change the regression coefficients very much.

MATHEMATICAL NOTES

Mathematical Note 2A

Notation and Description of Model

W_0, base wage (i.e., wage rate per hour in the absence of fatigue)

W, observed 'wage rate' (average hourly earnings)

H, hours worked per week

H_N, hours worked if base wage rate was paid at all levels of hours (i.e., in the absence of the fatigue effect)

H^*, hours estimated from W

$\hat{H}$, hours estimated from W, and by ignoring the effect of fatigue on the price of leisure

$Y = W_0 F(H)$, weekly money income [$F(H) = H$ in the absence of fatigue effect]

$Y_H = W_0 F'(H)$, price of leisure [$F'(H) = 1$ in the absence of fatigue; $F'(H) = 0$ at that level of hours which maximizes income]

$E_{X,Y}$, elasticity of X with respect to Y

$\bar{E}_{X,Y}$, partial elasticity of X with respect to Y

Constant elasticity demand function: $H = aI^b(Y_H)^c$. Two variants are examined: Model A: $I = W_0$; Model B: $I = Y$. In the analysis that follows it is assumed that there will be a positive price effect and a negative income effect on hours of work from a rise in the wage rate and that the income effect will be stronger than the substitution effect; i.e., in the absence of fatigue, higher wages will lead to shorter hours.

Model *A*

$$I = W_0$$
$$H_N = aW_0^{b+c}$$

Model *B*

$$I = Y$$

$$H_N = a(W_0 H_N)^b (W_0)^c = aW_0^{b+c} (H_N)^b = a^{1/1-b} W_0^{\frac{b+c}{1-b}}$$

I. *A* $H = aW_0^{b+c} (F'(H))^c = H_N (F'(H))^c$

Since $0 < F'(H) < 1$, and $c > 0$, $H < H_N$.

I. *B* $H = a(W_0 F(H))^b (W_0 F'(H))^c = H_N \left(\dfrac{F(H)}{H}\right)^b (F'(H))^c$

$$\frac{F'(H)}{F(H)/H} = E_{Y,H}$$

is probably less than 1; but $|b|$ is expected to be greater than c, so the result is indeterminate. For long hours of work where $E_{Y,H}$ is low (say 1/5), hours of work would be curtailed by fatigue unless the income elasticity is much greater than the price elasticity.

II. *A* $E_{H_N},W_0 = b + c$

$$\frac{dH}{dW} = (b+c) \frac{H}{W} + \frac{cH}{F'(H)} (F''(H)\frac{dH}{dW_0})$$

$$E_{H,W_0} = \frac{b+c}{1-cE_{F'(H),H}}.$$

Since $E_{F'(H),H} < 0$, $\left| E_{H_N},w_0 \right| > \left| E_{H,W_0} \right|$.

II. *B* $E_{H_N},W_0 = b + c/1 - b$

$$\frac{dH}{dW_0} = (b+c) \frac{H}{W_0} + \frac{(H)}{F(H)} \frac{dF(H)}{dH} \frac{dH}{dW_0} + \frac{cH}{F'(H)} \frac{dF'(H)}{dH} \frac{dH}{dW_0}$$

$$E_{H,W_0} = \frac{b+c}{1-bE_{F(H),H}-cE_{F'(H),H}}$$

$$= \frac{b+c}{1-b-\left[bE_{\frac{F(H)}{H},H} + cE_{F'(H),H}\right]},$$

so that $\left| E_{H_N} W_0 \right| > \left| E_{H,w_0} \right|$ unless $|b|$ is considerably greater than c.

III. (A and B) $\dfrac{H^*}{H} = \left(\dfrac{W}{W_0}\right)^{b+c} = \left(\dfrac{F(H)}{H}\right)^{b+c} > 1$

(since $\dfrac{F(H)}{H} < 1$ and $b + c < 0$).

IV. (A and B) $E_{H,W} = \dfrac{E_{H,W_0}}{E_{W,W_0}} = \dfrac{E_{H,W_0}}{1 + \bar{E}_{\hat{W},H} E_{H,W_0}}$,

so $|E_{H,W}| < |E_{H,W_0}|$

(since $\bar{E}_{W,H}$ and E_{H,W_0} are < 0).

V. A $\hat{H} = a(W)^b (W)^c = a W_0^{b+c} \left(\dfrac{F(H)}{H}\right)^{b+c}$

$\left(\dfrac{F(H)}{H}\right)^{b+c} > L, \hat{H} > H_N$

$H = H_N (F'(H))^c, H < H_N$ so $H < \hat{H}$

$\hat{H} > H_N > H$

V. B $\hat{H} = a(WH)^b (W)^c = a W_0^{b+c} \left(\dfrac{F(H)}{H}\right)^{b+c} (H)^b$

$= H_N \left(\dfrac{F(H)}{H}\right)^{b+c}$ so again, $\hat{H} > H_N$

$H = H_N \left(\dfrac{F(H)}{H}\right)^b (F'(H))^c; \hat{H} = H(E_{F(H),H})^c$

Since $0 < c, E < 1, \hat{H} > H$ (even if $H > H_N$)

VI. A $E_{H,W} = \dfrac{E_{H,W_0}}{1 + \bar{E}_{W,H} E_{H,W_0}}$

$= \dfrac{E_{H_N,W_0}}{1 - c E_{F',(H),H} + \bar{E}_{W,H} E_{H_N,W_0}}$,

so $\left| E_{H,W} \right| < \left| E_{H_N,W_0} \right|$

158

VI. $B\,E_{H,w} = \dfrac{E_{H,w_0}}{1+E_{\bar{w},H}E_{H,w_0}} = \dfrac{E_{H_N,w_0}(1-b)}{1-bE_{F(H),H}-cE_{F,(H)}+(b+c)E_{w,H}}$

$\qquad = \dfrac{(1-b)\,E_{H_N,w_0}}{1-b-c[E_{E_{F(H),H}},H]}$

Thus, if $E_{F(H),H}$ is a declining function of H, $|E_{H,w}| < |E_{H_N,w_0}|$ regardless of the relative sizes of b and c.

Mathematical Note 2B

Notation

Y = annual consumption or income (assumed constant over lifetime)
H = annual hours of work or study (————————————————)
P = years of life
W = hourly wage rate
S = hours of schooling
* = superscript indicating optimal
r = rate of interest (assumed constant)
ε = elasticity of W with respect to S
η = elasticity of Y with respect to H

W is a function of S. The individual maximizes Y at each level of H. Years before school age and after retirement are ignored.
 Then, if $r = 0$

$$Y = W\left(\frac{HP-S}{P}\right)$$

$$\frac{dY}{dS} = \left(H-\frac{S}{P}\right)W_s-\frac{W}{P}, \text{ setting } \frac{dY^*}{dS}=0,\; S^* = HP-\frac{W^*}{W^*_s}$$

$$\varepsilon^* = \frac{S^*}{HP-S^*}$$

$$Y^* = W^*\left(\frac{HP-S^*}{P}\right)\left(=\frac{W^{*2}}{W^*_s P}\right)$$

$$\frac{dY^*}{dH} = Y^*_H + \frac{dY^*}{dS}\frac{dS}{dH} = Y_H = W^*$$

159

$$Y^*/H = W^* - \frac{W^* S^*}{PH}; \quad \eta^* = \frac{HP}{HP - S^*} = 1 + \varepsilon^*$$

If $r > 0$,

$$Y = \frac{WH(e^{r(P-S/H)} - 1)}{e^{rP} - 1}$$

$$\frac{dY}{dS} = \frac{Y}{W} W_S - \frac{rWe^{r(P-S/H)}}{e^{rP}-1} \quad \text{or}$$

$$e^{r\left(P - \frac{S^*}{H}\right)} = \frac{W^*_S H}{W^*_S H - rW^*} = \frac{\varepsilon^*}{\varepsilon^* - \frac{rs^*}{H}}$$

$$\varepsilon^* = \frac{\dfrac{rS^*}{H} e^{r\left(P - \frac{S^*}{H}\right)}}{e^{r\left(P-\frac{S^*}{H}\right)} - 1}; \quad \left[Y^*_S = \frac{rW^{*2} H}{(W^*H - rW^*)(e^{rP}-1)}\right]$$

$$\frac{dY^*}{dH} = Y_H + \frac{dY}{dS^*} \frac{dS}{dH} = Y_H = \frac{W\left[e^{r(P-S/H)}\left(1 + \frac{rS}{H}\right) - 1\right]}{e^{rP} - 1}$$

$$E_{Y^*,H} = \eta = 1 + \varepsilon$$

Examples

If $W = aS^b$ where a and b are constants, then $\eta = 1 + \varepsilon = 1 + b$ for all rates of interest. However, the level of income will vary with r, and with the other parameters.

Let $r = 0, P = 60, a = 1, b = 1/2$

$$Y = S^{1/2}\left(H\frac{-S}{60}\right); \quad S^* = 20H \text{ (i.e. } \frac{S^*}{H} = 20 \text{ years of school)}$$

$$W^* = 2\sqrt{5} H$$

and $Y^* = 4/3 \sqrt{5} H^{3/2}$.

Let $r = 1, P = 60, a = 1, b = 1/2$

160

$$Y = S^{1/2} \frac{H(e^{(6 - \frac{S}{10H})} - 1)}{e^6 - 1}; \quad e^{6 \frac{S^*}{-10H}} = \frac{1}{1 - \frac{S^*}{5H}}$$

$\frac{S}{H} \cong 5$ (showing a high responsiveness of schooling to the rate of interest)

$W \cong \sqrt{5} \, H^{1/2}$ (one-half the wage rate at zero interest)

$Y \cong \frac{\sqrt{5}}{\sqrt{e}} H^{3/2}$ (less than half the income level at zero interest.)

Mathematical Note 2C

Notation

D, distance traveled

S, speed

T, travel time

F, travel fare

F*, fare per mile

W, hourly wage

H, hours of paid work

X, $WH - F =$ income or consumption

Z, $H + T = K - L$ (leisure) = a constant

$Z = $ constant, $U_H = U_T$

$$W = G(D); \quad F^* = F_1(S); \quad S = \frac{D}{T}$$

X is to be maximized

$$X = WH - F + \lambda_1 (W - G(D)) + \lambda_2 \left(F - DF^* \left(\frac{D}{T}\right)\right) +$$

$$\lambda_3 (Z - H - T)$$

$$X_W = H + \lambda_1 = 0; \quad X_D = -\lambda_1 W_D - \lambda_2 \left(F^* + \frac{D}{T} F^*_D\right) = 0$$

$$X_H = W - \lambda_3 = 0$$

$$X_F = -1 + \lambda_2 = 0 \quad X_T = \lambda_2 \frac{D^2}{T^2} F^*{}_{\frac{D}{T}} - \lambda_3 = 0$$

Then $\lambda_1 = -H$
$\lambda_2 = 1$
$\lambda_3 = W$

and: $HW_D - F^* - \frac{D}{T} F^*{}_{\frac{D}{T}} = 0; \frac{D^2}{T^2} F_{\frac{D}{T}} - W = 0$

Satisfying the left-hand equation assures us that the increase in labor income achieved by commuting an additional mile equals the increase in fare necessary to travel the greater distance in the same time.

The right-hand equation requires that the cost of saving us a unit of time by higher speed is equal to the wage rate.

Example

Some implications of this model may be seen more clearly with a simple example:

Let $W = bD^e$ and $F^x = cS^r$

Then we can derive from the preceding equations:

$WT = rFD$ (right-hand equation); $\dfrac{eWH}{D} - F = rF$ (left-hand equation)

Then $T = Z \dfrac{er}{er+r+1}$; $S = \left[\left(\dfrac{Zer}{er + r + 1} \right)^e \dfrac{b}{rc} \right]^{1/r-e+1}$

$D = \left[\left(\dfrac{Zer}{er+r+1} \right)^{r+1} \dfrac{b}{rc} \right]^{1/r-e+1}$

Note that D and S are positively related to b and negatively to c, but that T is not related to either. T *is* positively related to e *and* r.

162

$$\frac{dX^*}{dH} = X^*_H, \text{ and } E^*_{X,H} = X^*_H; \frac{H}{X^*} = \frac{W^*H}{W^*H - F^*}, \text{ but}$$

(from $eWH - F = rF$), this reduces to $E^*_{X,H} = \dfrac{r+1}{r+1-e}$

Note that this elasticity is greater than one, is not affected by b, c, or z, but is positively related to e, and negatively to r.

Mathematical Note 5A

The Relationship Between Property Income and Total Money Income in Equation B-4

Let P = property income, M = money income. Other symbols are explained in the text.

$$L = a + bY' + cP(L)' + dP(R)'; \quad Y' = \frac{wh + P(L) \cdot L + P}{\alpha + \beta P(L)};$$

$$\alpha + \beta P(L) = I$$

$$\frac{L}{\delta Y'} = b; \quad \frac{\delta h}{\delta Y'} = \frac{-\delta L}{\delta Y} = -b.$$

$$\frac{\delta h}{\delta P} = \frac{\delta h}{\delta Y'} \cdot \frac{\delta Y'}{\delta P} = \frac{-b}{I}$$

If $b^* = \dfrac{\delta L}{\delta Y'} \quad \dfrac{Y'}{L}$

$$\frac{\delta h}{\delta P} = \frac{-b^* L}{Y'I} = \frac{-b^* L}{wh + P(L) \ L + P} = \frac{-b^* L}{w(K\text{-}Lue) + P}$$

$$= \frac{-b^*}{w\left(\dfrac{K}{L} - ue\right) + \dfrac{P}{L}}$$

$$M = wh + P$$

$$\frac{\delta M}{\delta P} = w \frac{\delta h}{\delta P} + 1 = \frac{-b^*}{\dfrac{K}{L} - ue + \dfrac{P}{Lw}} + 1$$

$$= \left[-b^* + \frac{K}{L} - ue + \frac{P}{Lw} \cdot \frac{w(K\text{-}Lue) + P}{wL} \right]. \text{ Since we are analyz-}$$

ing the effects of introducing P, this statement reduces to:

Mathematical Note 5 B

$$\frac{\delta M}{\delta P} < 0 \text{ if } b^* + ue > \frac{K}{L}$$

$\frac{K}{L}$ is between 1.4 and 1.5 throughout, so that

$$\frac{\delta M}{\delta P} < 0 \text{ if } b^* > 1.5 \text{ (since } ue > 0)$$

Analysis of Biases in the Single-Equation Estimation of the Supply of and the Demand for Hours of Work

Writing variables in terms of their deviation from the means, one obtains these normal equations:

Supply: $m_{wH} = b_1 m_{HH} = c_1 m_{pH} = m_{u1H}$

$\qquad\quad m_{wp} = b_1 m_{Hp} + c_1 m_{pp} + m_{u1p}$

Demand: $m_{wH} = b_2 m_{HH} + c_2 m_{HF} + d_2 m_{HS} + m_{u2H}$

$\qquad\quad m_{wF} = b_2 m_{HF} + c_2 m_{FF} + d_2 m_{FS} + m_{u2F}$

$\qquad\quad m_{wS} = b_2 m_{HS} + c_2 m_{FS} + d_2 m_{ss} + m_{u2s}$

Circled values expected to be (but are not exactly) equal to zero. Let small letters represent observed values and capital letters with a hat represent two equation estimates. Then, one would expect:

$$\hat{B}_1 = \frac{\begin{vmatrix} m_{wH} - m_{u1H} & m_{Hp} \\ m_{wp} & m_{pp} \end{vmatrix}}{\Delta_1} = b_1 - \frac{m_{pp}m_{u1H}}{\Delta_1}$$

$$\hat{C}_1 = \frac{\begin{vmatrix} m_{HH} & m_{wH} - m_{u1H} \\ m_{Hp} & m_{wp} \end{vmatrix}}{\Delta_1} = c_1 + \frac{m_{Hp}m_{u1H}}{\Delta_1}$$

$$\hat{B}_2 = \frac{\begin{vmatrix} m_{wH} - m_{u2H} & m_{HF} & m_{HS} \\ m_{wF} & m_{FF} & m_{FS} \\ m_{wS} & m_{FS} & m_{ss} \end{vmatrix}}{\Delta_2} = b_2 - m_{u2H} \frac{\begin{vmatrix} m_{FF} & m_{FS} \\ m_{FS} & m_{ss} \end{vmatrix}}{\Delta_2}$$

$$\hat{C}_2 = \frac{\begin{vmatrix} m_{HH} & m_{wH} - m_{u2H} & m_{HS} \\ m_{HF} & m_{wF} & m_{FS} \\ m_{HS} & m_{wS} & m_{ss} \end{vmatrix}}{\Delta_2} = c_2 + m_{u2H} \frac{\begin{vmatrix} m_{HF} & m_{FS} \\ m_{HS} & m_{ss} \end{vmatrix}}{\Delta_2}$$

164

$$\hat{D}_2 = \frac{\begin{vmatrix} m_{HH} & m_{HF} & m_{wH} - m_{u2H} \\ m_{HF} & m_{FF} & m_{wF} \\ m_{HS} & m_{Fs} & m_{wS} \end{vmatrix}}{\Delta_2} = d_2 - m_{u2H} \frac{\begin{vmatrix} m_{HF} & m_{FF} \\ m_{HS} & m_{FS} \end{vmatrix}}{\Delta_2}$$

One may then use the estimates of cross products of deviation from the mean in our sample to solve these equations. In this sample, they supported the conclusions given on pp. 129 of the text.

Mathematical Note 5 C

Construction of a Price Index for Leisure Activity

Let i   = the ith activity

     L_i = total time spent on i

     R_i = total quantity of market goods used in i

     $P(\ )$ = price of

Then:

$$\frac{P(A_i)^1}{P(A_i)^0} = \frac{P(L)^1 L_i^0 + P(R)_i^1 R_i^0}{P(L)^0 L_i^0 + P(R)_i^0 R_i^0} \quad \text{the price relative}$$

But $\Sigma L_i = L_A$, where L_A is the amount of leisure time devoted to recreation,

$$\frac{P(L)^0 L_A^0}{P(L)^0 L_A^0 + \Sigma P(R)_i^0 R_i^0} \quad \text{has been measured as approximately equal to 0.9,}$$

and

$$\frac{\Sigma P(R)_i^1 R_i^0}{\Sigma P(R)_i^0 R_i^0} = \frac{P(R)_1}{P(R)_0}$$

Then: the price index

$$\frac{P(A)^1}{P(A)^0} = \frac{.9 P(L)^1}{P(L)^0} + \frac{.1 P(R)^1}{P(R)^0}$$

Mathematical Note 5D

Mathematical Analysis for Section 5.7

Write (1) $R = A \left(\dfrac{R}{A} \right)$

165

Then an increase in the demand for R may be regarded as the sum of an 'expansion' effect, arising out of an increase in A, and a 'substitution' effect arising out of an increase in the amount of R used per unit of A.

Thus:

$$(2) \ dR = \frac{\delta R}{\delta A} \ dA + \frac{\delta R}{\delta.\left(\dfrac{R}{A}\right)} \ d\left(\frac{R}{A}\right)$$

or

$$(3) \ dR = \frac{R}{A} \ dA + A \ d\left(\frac{R}{A}\right)$$

Similar reasoning leads to:

$$(4) \ dL = \frac{L}{A} \ dA + Ad\left(\frac{L}{A}\right)$$

We will be interested initially in two relations (P(L) is held constant in both).[1]

$$(5) \ \frac{dR}{dP(R)} = \frac{R}{A} \frac{\delta A}{\delta P(R)} = A \ \frac{\delta\left(\dfrac{R}{A}\right)}{\delta P(R)}$$

and

$$(6) \ \frac{dL}{dP(R)} = \frac{L}{A} \frac{\delta A}{\delta P(R)} + A \ \frac{\delta\left(\dfrac{L}{A}\right)}{\delta P(R)}$$

We turn first to the substitution effects (A as well as P(L) held constant).

$$(7) \quad A \ \frac{\delta\left(\dfrac{R}{A}\right)}{\delta P(R)} = \frac{\delta R}{\delta P(R)}$$

and

$$(8) \quad A \ \frac{\delta\left(\dfrac{L}{A}\right)}{\delta P(R)} = \frac{\delta L}{\delta P(R)}$$

1. P(L) and P(R) may be interpreted here as relative prices.

166

We continue to use the definition of x as the elasticity of substitution in leisure activity of R with respect to L:

$$(9) \quad x = \frac{\delta\left(\dfrac{R}{L}\right)}{\delta\left(\dfrac{P(R)}{P(L)}\right)} \frac{L\,P(R)}{R\,P(L)}$$

Moreover, since the consumer is assumed to be attempting to maximize A subject to a budget constraint, it would seem reasonable to expect that, at a given level of A:

$$(10) \quad \frac{\delta L}{\delta R} = \frac{-P(R)}{P(L)}$$

If P(L) as well as A is held constant;

$$(11) \quad x = \frac{\delta\left(\dfrac{R}{L}\right)}{\delta\,P(R)} \frac{L\,P(R)}{R} = \frac{L\,P(R)}{R}\left[\frac{\delta R}{\delta P(R)} - R\frac{\delta L}{\delta P(R)}\right]$$

$$= \frac{P(R)}{R}\left[\frac{\delta R}{\delta P(R)} - \frac{R}{L}\frac{\delta L}{\delta P(R)}\right]$$

Using (10):

$$(12) \qquad \frac{\delta R}{\delta P(R)} = \frac{-\delta L}{\delta P(R)} \frac{P(L)}{P(R)} \quad \text{or}$$

$$(13) \qquad \frac{\delta L}{\delta P(R)} = \frac{-\delta R}{\delta P(R)} \frac{P(R)}{P(L)}$$

Then (11) may be solved either as:

$$(14) \qquad X = \frac{\delta R}{\delta P(R)} \frac{P(R)}{R}\left[1 + \frac{\bar{R}}{\bar{L}}\right]$$

or

$$(15) \qquad X = \frac{-\delta L}{\delta P(R)} \frac{P(R)}{L}\left[1 + \frac{\bar{L}}{\bar{R}}\right]$$

Using the relationship

$$(16) \qquad A\,P(A) = L\,P(L) + R\,P(R) \quad (\text{or } \bar{A} = \bar{L} + \bar{R})$$

(14) and (15) may be written respectively as:

(17)
$$\frac{\delta R}{\delta P(R)} = \frac{R}{P(R)} \frac{\bar{L} x}{\bar{A}}$$

and

(18)
$$\frac{\delta L}{\delta P(R)} = \frac{-L}{P(R)} \frac{\bar{R}}{\bar{A}} X$$

Let us turn next to the expansion effects:

$$\left(\frac{R}{A} \frac{\delta A}{\delta P(R)} \text{ and } \frac{L}{A} \frac{\delta A}{\delta P(R)} . \text{See equations} (5) \text{and} (6) \right)$$

The demand for A might be regarded as a function

(19)
$$A = A(Y, P(A))$$

Holding real income, Y, constant.

(20)
$$\frac{\delta A}{\delta P(R)} = \frac{\delta A}{\delta P(A)} \frac{\delta P(A)}{\delta P(R)}$$

We may rewrite equation (16) as:

(21)
$$P(A) = \frac{L}{A} P(L) + \frac{R}{A} P(R)$$

Then:

(22)
$$\frac{\delta P(A)}{\delta P(R)} = \frac{R}{A}$$

and

(23)
$$\frac{\delta A}{\delta P(R)} = \frac{R}{A} \frac{\delta A}{\delta P(A)}$$

The expansion effects in equation (5) and (6) may then be written, respectively, as:

(24)
$$\frac{R}{A} \frac{\delta A}{\delta P(R)} = \frac{R^2}{A^2} \frac{\delta A}{\delta P(A)}$$

and

(25)
$$\frac{L}{A} \frac{\delta A}{\delta P(R)} = \frac{LR}{A^2} \frac{\delta A}{\delta P(A)}$$

168

Combining the expansion and substitution effects (but still holding P(L) and Y constant):

$$(26) \quad \frac{dR}{dP(R)} = \frac{R}{A}\frac{\delta A}{\delta P(R)} + A\frac{\delta\left(\frac{R}{A}\right)}{\delta P(R)} = \left(\frac{R}{A}\right)^2 \frac{\delta A}{\delta P(R)}$$

$$+ \frac{R}{P(R)}\frac{\bar{L}x}{\bar{A}}$$

and

$$(27) \quad \frac{dL}{dP(R)} = \frac{L}{A}\frac{\delta A}{\delta P(R)} + A\frac{\delta\left(\frac{L}{A}\right)}{\delta P(R)} = \frac{RL}{A^2}\frac{\delta A}{\delta P(A)}$$

$$- \frac{L}{P(R)}\frac{\bar{R}x}{\bar{A}}$$

Putting equations (26) and (27) in the form of elasticities, we write:

$$(28) \quad E_{R,P(R)} = \frac{\bar{R}}{\bar{A}} E_{A,P(A)} + \frac{\bar{L}}{\bar{A}} x$$

and

$$(29) \quad E_{L,P(R)} = \frac{\bar{R}}{\bar{A}} E_{A,P(A)} - \frac{\bar{R}}{\bar{A}} x$$

A similar analysis will lead to the results:

$$(30) \quad E_{L,P(L)} = \frac{\bar{L}}{\bar{A}} E_{A,P(A)} + \frac{\bar{R}}{\bar{A}} x$$

and

$$(31) \quad E_{R,P(L)} = \frac{\bar{L}}{\bar{A}} E_{A,P(A)} - \frac{\bar{L}}{\bar{A}} x$$